Wondering Between Two Worlds: Awakening to the Living God

by Jim Conlon

Planetary People Press
www.becomingplanetarypeople.com

Planetary People Press
A Division of JTT Marketing LLC
562 Winthrop Road
Union, NJ 07083

Copyright ©2018 by Jim Conlon

All rights reserved. No part of this book may be reproduced, stored in a retrieval system, or transmitted in any form, or by any other means electronic, mechanical, photocopying, recording, or otherwise, without the written permission of Planetary People Publishing.

Please direct permissions requests to:
john@jttmarketing.com.

Printed in the United States of America

Conlon, Jim, 1936—
Wondering Between Two Worlds: Awakening to the Living God

Print ISBN: 978-0-692-08364-2

Praise for *Wondering Between Two Worlds*

Jim Conlon's closely interwoven poetry and prose awaken the reader to the beauty and wonders of Earth and cosmos, to the miracle of life and of being alive. His stories, memories, and reflections draw the reader toward the divine, through the mysteries and beauty of creation, to what Teilhard de Chardin so powerfully described as the "divine milieu," a milieu that reveals itself to eyes of love and hearts of fire.
—**Ursula King**, Institute for Advanced Studies, University of Bristol, England

Father Jim Conlon is a man dedicated to all people of the world, all creatures and all things. This book of short essays and poems is inspirational. I feel uplifted by it. It has straightened out my vision here and there, something I need every day. He writes as a Catholic priest with a wide-open mind. If you can look through that window with him, wherever you stand, you will see the world with fresh eyes.
—**Thomas Moore**, author of *Care of the Soul* and *Ageless Soul*

Ecopoetry provides the creative horizon for this collection of poems and inspiring words. The reader is invited to embrace a new synthesis transcending our inherited dualisms, so that we can rediscover the creative God at the heart of creation itself. A timely and inspiring resource from one who has devoted his entire life to the vision and inspiration of the new story.
—**Diarmuid O'Murchu**, author of *Incarnation: A New Evolutionary Threshold*

Jim Conlon has given us many books of prose. Now he turns to reflections through poetry. He shines forth with a vision of the great beauty and mystery in nature. At the same time, he shows his generous capacity to be attentive to human suffering. This mingling of beauty and compassion is arresting—something we need to cultivate in our times. This book provides such a path.
—**Mary Evelyn Tucker**, Yale Forum on Religion and Ecology

Jim Conlon's spirituality, as expressed in the poetry of *Wondering Between Two Worlds*, carries a reader into a glorious time, what Thomas Berry called the ecozoic era. Jim feels the divine presence in all the things of the universe and allows himself to be swept up in wonder. If you read these poems, you too will find yourself praying with Jim, both as you read and as you go forth through your days, surrounded by magnificence.
—**Brian Swimme**, co-author with Thomas Berry of *The Universe Story*

Seldom do you find so much beauty, hope, and wisdom all in one place! This is the wonderful fruit of Jim Conlon's full life of growing and changing—and passing on that growing and changing to so many of the rest of us. We—and creation itself—are all the grateful beneficiaries.
—**Richard Rohr, O.F.M.**, Center for Action and Contemplation, Albuquerque, New Mexico

~TABLE OF CONTENTS~

Introduction	9
Prayer	19
Stories	45
Creativity	77
Nature	103
Beauty	119
Mystery	135
Hope	147
Mercy	169
Gratitude	181
Presence	203
Engagment	221
Geo-Justice	239
About the Author	265

∽DEDICATION∽

To Trina McCormick and Theresa Linehan and the staff of Springbank.

These women bring beauty to the world through clay, color, and word. They befriend the Earth and accomplish their great work by beautifying Springbank Retreat for Ecology and the Arts, where they welcome sacred seekers from around the world who journey there for rest and prayer and to reimagine the future.

INTRODUCTION

A Pilgrim's Prayer

Creator God,
source of love and life,
be with us now
as we venture forth.

May all our days be flooded
with precious gifts
and great anticipation,
enveloped with fresh energy.

May we discover
new doorways,
opening to the unfinished journey
that awaits us.

A Pilgrim Wandering Between Two Worlds

We are pilgrims of the future, grounded in anticipation of a world that will be ever-unfinished. This vantage point on the universe invites us to become people of beauty, people who embrace an exquisite balance between novelty and continuity. We are challenged to experience the depths, magnitude, and magnificence of existence, to become more and more alive to the potential before us.

The way ahead will be prompted by a fresh awareness that there is still much for us to do, and that we live at a time filled with opportunities to become a people of the future. As people on this journey of abundance, we dive deeply to explore the ocean of grace we dare to call our life.

We awaken to each new moment and become aware that our world is not static or stuck; rather, it is a swirling upstart spring that is expansive, invigorating, curious, and open to what is next. On this journey, we venture forth toward an integral life founded on two faiths: faith in God and faith in Earth. With this view, we focus on what lasts, and we delve into the inexhaustible depths of what we call God.

We take up the challenge as people of two faiths to reconcile and synthesize the religious zeal of our Christian tradition with the emergence of the new cosmic story. It is a story that invites the practice of a profound cosmic patience and anticipation, as each new chapter in the story unfolds.

The pilgrim's journey, as she wanders between two worlds, moves forward in reconciling our trust in God and Earth so that it becomes trust in God in and through Earth. This trust is woven together in a tapestry that is religiously forward looking, yet unfinished and sensitive as we navigate the world through shared images, stories, and symbolic languages.

We peer attentively into the silent depths of a vast well of wisdom, wherein all things feel soaked in the sacred. We realize anew that our experience is derived from an immersion in the great new story.

With Canadian Chief Dan George, we become aware that "We are alive as much as we keep the Earth alive." This aliveness is overflowing with insight, breath, zest, reverence, awe, wonder, liberation, love, and the fullness of life.

With St. Augustine, we cry out with hope, which is the mother of anger and courage. This time in history can be understood as an apostatic time, when at first glance we seem to be embarking on a journey into nothingness, a time when there do not appear to be any answers to our enduring questions. Words fail us as we ascend to a place where life is once again magnificent.

A new time of ecopoetics is rising on the horizon. Seekers from many regions and backgrounds and with many perspectives are putting the promptings of their hearts into words. Their words flow from the deep ecological imprint in their souls into images and stories that connect art, politics, and Earth. Their poetry penetrates the psyche and heart to transform us and give birth to a new world that is fresh, unfinished, and entirely new.

A new era is upon us, calling forth each of us to ponder the intersection of sacred trust and the amazing universe. As we wander between two worlds, it is time to offer our ecopoetic response.

We Remember and Give Thanks

We remember and give thanks:
> For the gift of unique differences present in God's creation—every color, culture, gender and creed; every flower, tree and creature who manifests the beauty of difference and dissolves all tendencies to make the world the same.

We remember and give thanks:
> For being born into an interconnected world where relationships are the very essence of existence, and for the opportunity to create community and heal all brokenness, should it become manifest in families, communities, politics and culture.

We remember and give thanks:
> For the capacity for intimacy and sensitivity that we gratefully express in our relationships with self, neighbors, Earth and the divine.

We remember and give thanks:
> For the capacity and possibility to bring more beauty to the world, especially where it is most needed regarding Earth, society and soul.

We remember and give thanks:
> For the gift of openness that offers new possibilities as they shine forth in unplanned surprises that show up on our paths not yet taken.

We remember and give thanks:
> For the opportunity to lend our gifts to support the ongoing, unfolding dynamics of the great work of our time, as available to us through the gifts of culture, society and soul.

We remember and give thanks:
> For solitude and engagement that make it possible to be attentive to the sacred impulses that emerge into fresh awareness and prompt us into action.

We remember and give thanks:
> For the gift of creativity, those resurrection moments occur when dreams rise up in our imagination and take residence beyond conscious thought. May these guiding stars continue to reveal the call within the call, as we become liberated from patterns of the past and venture forth beyond trodden paths and give our gifts to the world in as-yet-unimagined ways.

We remember and give thanks:
> That when we do good works, we are aligning our gifts to the dream of the Earth.

We remember and give thanks:
> That the work we are called to do is not good because it will turn out well, but rather because it is worth doing.

We remember and give thanks:
> For the challenges that each day presents when we embrace patience, ambiguity and risk, knowing that somehow we are on the path of gratitude and praise.

We remember and give thanks
> That our greatest gift in what we are called to do in this life is to make our contribution to what remains unlived and unfinished on our journey.

We remember and give thanks:
> As we reflect on our journey and ponder the origins of the universe, and its unique unfolding in time, and gain a glimpse of the future still unfinished before us.

~PRAYER~

Prayer Is a Noun

Prayer is a noun. To pray is a verb.
Prayer happens when we gaze, bathe, soak, listen.
When we pray, we become enveloped in the divine presence.
To pray can be understood as engaging to be freed from an unlived life.
To pray is to notice, pay attention, tell our story and the story of the universe.
To pray is to be grateful, embrace mystery, become unselfconscious.
To pray is to encounter, imagine, experience beauty.
To pray is to embrace solitude, to wonder.
Prayer happens as we engage in justice, dialogue,
become one with an experience of beauty.
Pray, dream, live the question, have an emotional moment.
In prayer, become curious, become a prophet, a mystic, experience a spark of grace, see God in all things.

Prayer Happens

Thomas Merton encourages us to pray; however, he does not tell us how.

Others offer more clues. Mary Oliver says, "I don't know exactly what a prayer is. I do know how to pay attention." These words remind us that prayer comes from noticing what is all around us.

Meister Eckhart says prayer is about gratitude: "If the only prayer you say in your life is 'thank you,' that would suffice."

When we pray with intention, we are empowered to accomplish the things for which we pray. Prayer happens when we ponder a passage from scripture; gaze upon the beauty of creation; or experience the enveloping presence of the divine as fully present in every plant, flower and tree.

Meister Eckhart speaks again: "If I spent enough time with the tiniest creature, even a caterpillar, I would never have to prepare a sermon, so full of God is every creature."

Portuguese poet Sophia de Mello-Breyner Andresen names the deep mystery of prayer when she writes, "I'm listening, but I don't know if what I hear is silence or God."

For many, our formative years were framed by a formal approach to prayer. Perhaps today your prayer has evolved and you have a more felt sense of the sacred.

We can say that because justice is constitutive of the gospel, justice-making is itself a prayer. Justice can be understood as a moment of grace in which the walls between the secular and the sacred dissolve, and we enter a new experience in which everything is holy.

Prayer happens when we listen to the cry of the poor and say, "I saw Christ today," or when we experience the cry of the Earth as we witness climate change in floods, fires, hurricanes and drought.

Prayer happens when we imagine ourselves being carried forward by a profound awareness of God in all things and all things in God.

Black Mountain Prayer

Fourteen in number, we sit in a circle,
wise women whose cultures are many.

On the journey of rest and letting go,
we hail from Nigeria, Peru, New Zealand,
Australia, America, Canada, Micronesia.

Hearing the stories of the people of Abraham,
we think, *Je me souviens*,
Recuerde, I remember.

In our circle of resurgent spirits,
the freedom songs of Exodus
echo in our souls.

Here in Maggie Valley,
whispered songs of letting go
invite the gaze of Jesus.

In this Black Mountain moment,
we open our hearts once again
in our quest for the living God.

Prayer to the Ancient One

Ancient One of ancient days,
creator of water, rock, fire and air,
mother of winged, finned, furred and legged,
sister of all who walk, swim and soar,
we thank you for the gifts of love and life.

Great Spirit, we raise our immolation to you on high,
and to every good companion down below.
On this October day,
we send our prayers to the sacred sky
and embrace all children here below.

Life of Prayer

Our approach to prayer reveals the in-between times we live in and reflects double-sided points of view. This was demonstrated by a friend who contributed the following comment in a conversation about prayer: "When I wake, I feel grateful; then I ask for stuff."

My early years, particularly my first years in the seminary, were days of inordinate self-consciousness. I understood prayer to be a time to scour the psyche and examine every thought and impulse that surfaced from the depths of the soul.

Over the years, I set aside the practices from those early days, which for the most part involved repetitive prayer. Now my prayer is more about the experience of awe and wonder that comes from looking around and drinking in the beauty and entrancement of the natural world, the spontaneity of a child or a rose about to blossom.

Now when I pray, I reflect on the profound insights of the mystics and prophets of yesterday and today. One of these is Thomas Merton, who summarizes the spiritual call of the true self to be transparent at the threshold of each encounter with the divine.

Over the years, my prayer life has changed. It has evolved from the family rosary to a later breviary, to a current immersion into the sea of the sacred, wherein words are replaced by an awareness of the divine beauty that surrounds and permeates all of life.

A Cosmologist's Prayer

I want to live like Earth lives,
dispensing bouquets of beauty all around,
to be alive, visionary and prophetic,
immersed in the wonder
and belonging of each new day.

May I be one who prays,
a therapist of the apathetic,
a vagabond of the obvious,
someone who delivers
each person to herself.

May I be a grateful person,
guided by story
and shared dream experience,
a cosmological subject,
an architect and practitioner
of those great cosmic gifts
of Earth, art and spirit.

May I be one who celebrates
the generosity of the sun,
the wisdom of each revelatory moment,
as paradox becomes
the instrument of truth and surprise.

May I be a good companion,
a source of creativity and compassion
for all who join us on the journey.

Now is the time, dear friends,
become a beacon of hope,
a source of fresh energy
and zest for life,
an author of what lies
deep in each tender soul.

May I be one who proclaims
the habits of my heart
through the practices
of clay, color, music and word,
and who makes the road itself
by walking through the cosmic gifts
and virtues of patience, ambiguity and risk.

May I become a cosmological person
who ventures forth
and discovers new ways of feeling,
and whose heart
discovers new ways of thinking.

As we become aware
that tomorrow will unfold
from the far reaches of the universe
into a new cultural genesis,
together we pray:
"May all beings be happy, may all beings be free."

Aho! Mitakuye oyasin.
Merci.
Deo gracias.
Gracias a Dios.

Blessed be.
Yes, blessed be.
Amen, Alleluia, Amen!

This is My Blood

Now, quenched and nourished by this great and generous moment, we venture forth to heal what is broken and renew the face of the Earth.

Together, we join our hands and hearts to make possible new and heroic acts that flow from mercy, justice and love.

We join our hands and hearts today and give thanks to the Ancient One of ancient days.

Nourished by food for the journey, we celebrate each new moment with signs of companionship and gestures of peace.

We honor the presence of the triune God.

We co-create the future, replete with harmony, balance and peace, as together we celebrate and say to the Earth and each other, "May the future be better than all the pasts."

Amen!

Rosary for the New Story

Prayer is joy, emptiness, wonder, imagination.
Prayer heals the soul with acts of justice.
Prayer is following the guidance of Rilke,
who tells us to love the questions themselves.

Prayer is joy, sorrow, creativity, change.
Prayer is pottery, painting, drumming, taiji.
Prayer is the openness to be like Teilhard,
a pilgrim of the future who is returning from the past.

Prayer is an act of the true self.
Prayer is the new story rising into action.

See More Clearly

My prayer is, as the song says,
"Love thee more dearly,
see thee more clearly,
day by day."

I pray amidst the sunshine and rain,
the solitude and pain,
to stop the bullets of violence
that pierce our hearts,
wound our minds,
cause upset in our souls.

Today is the time, dear friend.
Be like an astronaut
who views the world on high,
views the world as one,
no boundaries, no separation,
one body, one spirit,
one Earth, one home,
one place from which
to grow your soul.

Before Tomorrow Comes

Listen now
to the voice of the hidden one,
that one over there
in the back row,
over there, almost unseen.
Listen now again
and invite her to the front row.
Together let us sing and praise
before tomorrow comes.

Let Heaven

Come, wise and ineffable One,
embrace Your people.
Deep in the heart
of all You hold dear,
flower forth.
Petal me with goodness,
beauty and love.
Disclose what remains hidden.
Send forth Your spirit
to heal the wounds of Earth.
Heal the brokenhearted.
Make us one again,
holy without blemish.
Become the novelty
from which beauty flows,
with patterns that connect.
Let heaven happen now.

A Good Day

Walking by
on a crisp late December day,
I see wheelchairs, pushcarts.

Shuffling elders greet the day.
Will it be their last New Year?
I wonder.

I stop to review
the headlines in today's paper.

Along the way,
I enter a chapel
from the back street.

I gaze on Jesus
and wish our tattered world,
with confidence, Good day!

Teach Me

God of hope, mercy and peace,
Sacred One of sacred days,
unite what is broken,
renew the face of creation.

Teach me to live.
Teach me to give.

Sacred One of sacred days,
teach me about beauty,
about difference, about love.

Sacred One of sacred days,
awaken me to understand,
experience and embrace
God in all things.

Teach me,
that we may become people of hope,
people of mercy, people of peace.
Amen.

What It Means to Live

A cool, fresh morning
in South Carolina.
I pray today for freedom
from whatever blocks my spirit
or incarcerates my soul.

I pray for the freedom
to roam the far-off land,
to walk softly
in the sunshine and the rain.

Cleanse my heart, O Sacred One.
Illuminate my soul.

As I awaken today,
may I imagine once again
the meaning of my life,
know on this cool Carolina morning
what it means to live.

Max Comes Home

Springbank Retreat is a sacred place where women from around the world gather to renew their spirit, refresh their energy and reflect on the beauty of creation as they drink in the divine creativity that infuses their souls and all of life.

Among the Springbank community are a number of four-legged friends that Thomas Merton referred to as *saints*. One member of this canine community is a shy, beautiful creature called Max.

On occasion, Max likes to wander off the property. Once while I was staying at Springbank, Max disappeared on Easter Sunday. He did not return the next day. When he still had not appeared after several days, we began to wonder if some harm had befallen Max. We feared it was possible that he would never return.

On the Wednesday after that Easter, several of us were working on the community's prayer lodge. At the end of the day, I suggested we pray for Max and send out our energy for his safe return.

There were five of us. We joined hands and formed a circle, and began to pray. As energy flowed from hand to body to hand, we imagined a cone of energy surrounding us and extending to Max, wherever he might be. Our prayer was to cleanse, purify and protect him. We imagined the energy surrounding Max and inviting him home.

One member of our group said she could sense Max. She

assured us that he was alive. We concluded our prayer circle and went off into the night.

The next morning, we received good news: Max had come home and was enjoying an abundant breakfast. It seemed that our prayer had been answered. Our prayer for Max had invited him home.

A Great Amen

Now is the time
to claim my inheritance,
say how proud I am
to have lived in Canada.

I went to school there,
skipped grade three,
road the school bus,
attended high school.

I worked the streets
in Toronto and Chicago,
taught theology,
worked for justice.

I let go of pain,
went south to pray,
to celebrate each moment,
to say amen today.

God of the Cosmos

God of the cosmos,
blessed of the land,
I come before You today
to listen,
to celebrate,
to pray.

God of the cosmos,
blessed of the land,
we are welcome here.
Beauty heals our hearts
on this wondrous day.

Sisters, brothers, friends,
may each soul expand,
embrace the mystery of it all,
gaze upon the goodness of each day.

Mass for the Earth

Great and holy Mystery, we gather here today, with trust in our hearts, in this sacred place, at this altar of the Earth, where longing and terror lie.

Here in this world of beauty, we wonder and give thanks for the gift of Your creation.

We welcome all gathered at this moment. We bring hope and peace and promise to all and to every nation.

Today, at this incarnational moment, we tell the great story. We remember our origins and how all came about.

We come to You today, along with our ancestral companions, those good and gracious ones of yesterday who join us now and who make the two worlds one.

We announce the great narrative of our evolutionary lives.

We remember those early days when we emerged from the vast oceanic depths and blossomed forth into the unimaginable beauty that adorns this radiant planet.

This sacred rock where our altar stands today was formed from the elements. Wondrous beauty from the divine imagination formed mountains, flowers and creatures great and small.

We take these simple elements of bread and wine, conscious of this liberating moment of yesterday and today.

We take this bread as freedom for the land and as fuel for the journey, as together we say, "This is my body."

As we take this chalice of wine from the work of human hands, we dare to say, "This my blood."

~STORIES~

Seamless Story

I want to tell you about life,
about what it means to be human.

Guided by your inner compass,
discover your identity.

In the give and take of everyday existence
discover what it means to be human.

Some call it prayer, others call it self-awareness—
this guide that supports you on your journey.

Let its seamless story
guide your every action,
as the trajectory unfolds,
and each new moment
is filled with wisdom and surprise.

September Stories

Stories are amazing. They tell us who we are and why we're here; they provide a glimpse into the future and reveal where we may be going.

When we tell stories, we remember our origins, ponder our destiny and renew our purpose.

Stories are personal, religious and cosmic. They provide a context in which to celebrate the exaltation of existence, a context in which to consecrate sorrow as we compose a chorus of gratitude and praise joyfully our loving God.

As planetary people, we are all cousin and kin. We share a common story.

Each of us was present at the sacred moment of the great flaring forth. Hydrogen was cooked into helium. From within the great supernova, the elements were created, rocks formed, life burst forth and humanity was born and walked upon this sacred home we call Earth.

Startled by all this wonder, we joyfully awakened to the beauty of it all. We gave great thanks for the precious gift we call life.

Through the generosity of the great and magnanimous One we celebrate in this sacred September moment, we give thanks for the gift of self-reflexive consciousness. As a grace-filled people, we honor and proclaim the divine creative energy that permeates every person, puppy and place.

With an amazing exclamation, we proclaim to all who populate this sacred land, "Creation has become conscious of itself!"

We journey forward to replenish our souls and invigorate our hearts. We give thanks for this new resurrection moment.

We venture forth to reshape our lives, honor our ancestors and pay homage to the first nations of Earth.

With drums, flutes, clay and great hope for the future yet unborn, we anticipate each new tomorrow as we join good companions for the days ahead.

Confident that now is the time, we become awake and watchful for those sacred impulses that will guide us forward as we offer our gifts to this awesome and unfinished universe.

Stories Awaken Us

I have always loved stories. Stories tell of origins. They reveal where we are now and provide a glimpse of the future. A good story is engaging; it provides us with experiences of joy and of sorrow, and deepens meaning in our lives.

When we listen to a story or tell a story, we have an opportunity to take a fresh look at our lives. Each new moment becomes an opportunity to wonder about life and the magnificence that is available to us. Stories can awaken us to the sacredness of existence.

Stories can be about love and loss, people and events, memories of sacred awakenings and radical amazement, enduring hope, mystery and great trust.

Stories name our journey. They invite intimacy and dissolve projection and illusion as they introduce us to reality. When we tell stories, we find our voice, rediscover our identity and ignite flames of compassion and hope.

Anticipation

The world awaits us,
the future unfinished.

Plunge into an unknown,
unfolding new tomorrow.

Let the future happen now.
Listen deeply to its call.

Be patient.
Become empty.

Play your part
in the great cosmic drama.

Celebrate meaning, freedom.
Give birth to what has never happened.

When I Was Young

Tuesday morning,
a quiet winter day
on Signal Mountain
in Tennessee.
Today it's off to Nashville
to see "he shoots… he scores."

Memories abound
of ice on the rivers
and our frozen lawn.
Days across the miles
bring forth memories
of when we were young
and strong.

I peer now
from these far-off arena seats
to view the game
I practiced
when I was young.

My Sister Tells Our Family Story

Stories tell us who we are and where we've been. My sister Mary loved stories, especially our family's story. Often she would fly to Salt Lake City and pour through the historical records to connect the dots between us and our origins in County Armagh in Ireland.

A few years ago, when her interest was at its peak, she and I visited the farms and graveyards of our ancestors in Central and Southwestern Ontario in Canada. As we toured the home place of our ancestors, she recorded the data from their gravestones and baptismal records, and other information, and composed our family story.

The story of our Irish family began during the potato famine. Half of the family stayed in Ireland, while the other half sailed to Canada to escape the possibility of starvation.

My fondest memory of my sister's passion to tell our family story happened in 2003, on the occasion of our Conlon family reunion. It took place on a Saturday evening, at the Community Center in our hometown of Sombra. During that weekend, I was privileged to celebrate the liturgy at Sacred Heart Church in Port Lambton, the town where I was born.

During the homily, I talked about my father, who in his later years would sit on the front step of our family home and invite people to join him and tell him a story. I recalled how my mother, Elizabeth, would join other women in our town at the quilting bee. I suggested that each of us who gathered for the Conlon family reunion was like a patch in the Conlon quilt. We were patches from Alberta, New Hampshire, New Jersey, Delaware, California, Ontario and beyond.

I also said that our family was like Ezekiel in the Hebrew Bible. We had been driven into exile because the potato famine, and had come to Canada. I explained that our story can be told by the names and dates of our ancestors inscribed on the tombstones in the nearby cemetery. It is, you could say, a story told by the St. Clair River and by the first fall of snow that carpeted our town each winter.

At this reunion, we had come to our hometown—which was home to each of us and to our story. It was there that we first learned our Christian story and became people of faith.

During that weekend, my sister Mary shared her genesis story of the Conlon family. She told us how our ancestors came to Canada in 1840, how they found an area that reminded them of Ireland, and how they became lumber merchants so they could make a living and raise families in their newfound land.

As she recited the family genealogy that evening—our ancestral Book of Genesis—Mary joyfully recalled how, after writing to many people in Ireland she thought might be descendants of our ancestors, she had finally received a response. The letter confirmed her research and indelibly forged the connection to our Irish family roots. Following this discovery, she and I visited Ireland, met our relatives, and celebrated our family story.

Later, when Mary and I explored where the Conlons settled in Ontario, we saw that the landscape there was remarkably similar to the land they had left. We noticed that some of the gravestones of first cousins were next to each other in Ontario, yet their names were spelled differently. This suggested to me that those who immigrated were not highly literate.

Our Conlon family reunion in Port Lambton was a great weekend, and it closed with a talent show in which the children presented a play of the migration to Canada. When I left the hall that evening, I knew that something important and sacred had happened. I had learned again my family's story.

Recently, I listened to my cassette recording of Mary's presentation. I remembered how the room had been decorated with family photos that evoked images from her story. It is a story of the unstoppable spirit alive in the hearts of those adventurous souls who came to a new country, with hope for a land of opportunity. It is a story recorded in my Celtic genetic coding and inscribed in the St. Bridget's cross that hangs on the wall of my Berkeley home. It is a story of struggle and sacrifice, a story of adventures and new life.

It is a story that each of us can share in our own form—regardless of the particular origins that have shaped our lives and that have given us a sense of the sacred that feeds us hope.

Dare to Say

Tonight I present an invitation:
let your heart speak
about what until now seemed hidden,

perhaps an opening
to write down
what you did not yet dare to tell.

Sink below the tatters of your heart.
Speak of mystery,
of memories of a future made entirely in the past.

Just at this moment,
contemplate the emptiness,
listen to the deep unknown.

Be at peace.
Solve the unsolved questions
that you wonder about each day.

Questions Not Yet Asked

I wonder what it means, growing old.
Is it just about diminishment here and there,
about misplaced glasses and elusive keys—
to where did they disappear, this time?

No. As I look back over the gift of years,
I know it means more:
it means memories and stories as yet untold,
still waiting to be unlocked
by those young enough to ask about them.

Heart Song

There is a tear in my heart
that wants to cry
to a world devastated by loss,
loss of life, beauty and all we hold dear.

Yes, there's a tear in my heart,
a cry for beauty,
for flowers, mountain streams.
May all the children of the world
cry out from their depths.

Somewhere there's a song,
a lyrical presence bursting forth.
Beauty, rhythm and song,
the song in my heart.

A Moment in Black

Barack Obama,
president of these United States,
stood at the podium
on that special September day,
inaugurating the museum of
African American History and Culture.

A tear fell from his eye
as he told the American story
and his own.

My heart leapt with joy
to witness this great moment
with Sr. Martina of Nigeria.

Just for a moment,
a warm bipartisan time.
I heard the bell of freedom
pulsate in my heart
and resonate across
this sacred land.

Language Mystery

Symbols, images, stories,
unpredictable patterns.

Become a verb.
Immerse yourself
in the randomness of life.

Enter the abyss.
Become a story-telling soul,
weave wild imaginings.

Navigate the world.
Become people of the future,
consecrators of mystery yet untold.

Listen in silence to the thirst
for this once-sacred place.

Envelop yourself in a great narrative,
now seen more clearly
from a cosmic perspective.

Oneness

It is happening now,
a deep inclination
to live, to create, to merge.
Become one with love, unite.
Embrace the vastness,
ponder the stars,
merge into oneness.

It is oneness
that comes to me today,
inspired by Ernesto Cardinal
when he told the story
of the people of Solentiname.
It is a story of hope and companionship,
of liberation and breakthrough,
a story of what lies
at the floorboard of our soul.

Tale to Tell

My open door reveals a mess,
papers scattered everywhere.
"Nothing is ever lost,"
I hear someone say.

Yet at this very moment,
doubts rise in my soul.

"Look around.
See the pattern of your life,"
I hear a silent voice declare.

Discover a pattern in it all.
See life emerging,
a story yet untold.

Somewhere, these scribbled notes
have a tale to tell.
Perhaps there is order after all.

Endless Search

I saw God today,
sitting around a table,
sorting through a tangled maze
of papers and files
and more papers and files,
sending one more email,
adding one more name
to a seeming endless waiting list.

Unexpectedly, someone passes by.
The room erupts into applause
as a familiar seeker announces,
"I am on my way home."

Others round the table
manage a twinkle and smile.
They sign up for the next time,
to continue what sometimes
seems an endless search.

Grandfather Clock

Resting in my apartment in Berkeley,
I scan the images and artifacts,
each a memory from the past:
pictures of Richard and Elizabeth,
reminders of Ireland and New Zealand,
the Thomas Berry award,
photos of days in school:
grade school in Sombra,
classmates at St. Peter's,
teammates in baseball
at Corunna, Wilkesport, Waubuno and Wallaceburg.

As I immerse my mind
in memories and portraits of the past,
My eye focuses on the grandfather clock in the corner.

For a moment, I wonder about
the many hundred-year stories it can tell:
stories of organic time when my ancestors lived,
their lives guided by the seasons, by dawn and dusk,
by the creative wisdom of each emergent moment.

When we know our beginnings
and become aware of where we are now,
we are prompted by each new moment
calling us forward
into an as-yet-to-be-realized developmental future.

Liquid Recollections

As floods of memories emerge,
the shimmering beauty
of the St. Clair River
heals my soul.
Liquid recollections return
a bountiful harvest
of living memories.
Stories of sadness and joy
percolate through my awareness,
each a living memory
of enduring moments,
active in the past
yet alive today.
Moments of goodness and gratitude
offer glimpses of enduring peace.

One More Afternoon

My father was a fierce and generous man.
He left school after grade six
to cultivate his family's country farm.
He worked hard,
and retired late
to earn a modest pension for his labor.

Often in his later days,
my father would sit on our front porch.
He would visit with neighbors and tell stories.
Now on this August day,
I wish for one more afternoon with my father
on the front porch telling stories.

Coffins and Cribs

What a story
this small twig can tell,
lying gently in my hand.

This offspring of an oak
that once stood stately on Earth,
wood became lumber.

Making shelter for the homeless,
cribs for newborns,
coffins for those born again.

What a story
this small twig can tell.

Another Nativity Moment

Meister Eckhart often said
when talking about Christmas,
Why celebrate Jesus' birthday
a thousand years ago
if he is not born again
among us today?

On this day, Trina,
we celebrate
the memory of your birth
and the many incarnations
that continue in this sacred manger
we call Springbank.

Elephant Memories

A friend of mine told me this story some years ago. Once there was a man who lived and worked in Africa. It came to pass that he befriended a herd of elephants who had gathered in the area.

The elephants eventually wandered off into the jungle. Some time later, the man died.

Without any message or communication, the elephants traveled to the place where the man had lived. They remained there for some time, before returning to their natural habitat. Through some mysterious means, they knew of the passing of the man who had become their friend, and they went to mourn his passing.

I believe we have much to learn from our four-legged friends. Not only do humans have memories, but so do others among God's creatures with whom we share this planet. Such was the case with this herd of elephants.

This story reminds us that we are capable of nonverbal communication, and that we don't need words to create memories. Memory is a special gift. When we remember, we recall the formational moments of joy and sorrow, sunlight and showers, dawn and dusk, that mark each day.

One of the tragedies in life is when people lose their memories. When there is no memory, there is no story, no recollection of the sacred moments that have nourished our life.

The Other Side

Descend the road
leading to the dock.
Across the driveway,
hear the river splash below.

On the left, a sunken boat,
a place where fish
and polliwogs
frolic in the noon sun.

From the channel,
a freighter sounds its horn,
while eager passengers
board the waiting ferry,
in anxious anticipation
of their arrival to the other side.

Ocean of Grace

We gather today,
friends of Doug and Camille,
to launch and celebrate
a buoyant new beginning
on their journey.

Here on the shores
of the mighty Pacific,
may they be carried forward
into this new time.

May their new home
become a place
of wonder, belonging and love;
a sacred place where their lives flow
into new oceans of grace.

In this place where newness happens,
peace presides
as their blue boat home
sails confidently
into fresh adventures yet untold.

What Time Is It in the Universe?

Whenever I enter a jewelry store, instinctively I migrate to the display case that contains watches. I gaze at the Bulova, Rolex and others. In my mind's eye, I imagine myself with one of these fine timepieces on my wrist.

When I emerge from this timepiece trance and wander down the street, I ask myself why I'm so fascinated with and attracted to a watch. In that instant, my mind goes back to one evening in a cosmology class when the question was posed: "What time is it in the universe?"

As we reflected on our different understandings of time, one person spoke up: "There is circular time. This notion of time marks the recurring seasons: spring, summer, autumn and winter. There are also the dawn and dusk of each day." The rhythms of time are celebrated by monastic communities who chant Matins in the morning, Vespers in the evening and Compline at night.

We recall the words of Albert Einstein: "Time has no independent existence apart from the order of events by which we measure it."

There is also the notion of deep time, which can be understood as developmental time. From this perspective, we reflect on the transformational moment of each chapter in the great story about which Thomas Berry spoke, back to the origin of time—that moment of the great flaring forth when time began.

As I gaze at the decades-old wristwatch on my wrist to see what time it is today, I wonder what deep time story it has to tell. It is perhaps the story of the great live oak standing stately in the field, which I pass by every morning. It is also the story of the original supernova event, fourteen billion years ago, when out of nothingness, the elements emerged. Hydrogen and helium were cooked in the intense heat of the great flaring forth. The solar system came into being. In the planetary geological event, Earth was ushered into existence. This first chapter of the great universe story has been told by physicists and astronomers.

As the waters bathed planet Earth, life appeared. Then after a long generative time, beings with self-reflective consciousness rose up in Africa and walked upon the land. With the rise of consciousness came culture, language, story, the practice of fire building and the formation of habitat. These chapters are explained to us by biologists, anthropologists and others.

Ilia Delio says, "The embodied person that you are at this very moment—all the constituents that would eventually come together into the person that is you—was present at the Big Bang."

Reflecting on this progression of time, we remember that we are all members of and scribes for its great genealogical story. It is the story of our sacred origins, a narrative of our unfolding in time, and a revelatory tale that holds glimpses of the future.

This great deep time story provides a perspective and a context for the discovery of where we are now. It is a profound reminder that we belong here, and that we've always belonged here. The birds in the air, the fish in the sea and all who walked upon the Earth remind us that we are all cousin and kin.

It is in and through the universe story that it is possible to transcend the consumer-driven society in which we live today, and to become poets of each evolutionary moment who engage wholeheartedly in a joyful journey of destiny and purpose.

It is a thrilling realization that we are alive today, at this precise moment of collective destiny. As we celebrate the consciousness of a time developmental universe, we let go of any notion of a mechanistic, clockwork God. We sink instead into an awareness of the vast enveloping presence who calls us forward, with a profound realization that we were born into a time developmental universe.

With this awareness, we honor those who have come before. We become more deeply immersed in the unfolding of history that Thomas Berry referred to as "those overarching movements that give shape and meaning to life by relating the human venture to the larger destinies of the universe." We experience the magnetic intuition that calls us forward to experience the mysterious qualities of the universe. And we take to heart the words of Barack Obama, who said, "Change will not come if we wait for some other person or some other time."

As we look back in time, we seek explanations for the ecological devastation and cultural pathology we witness around us. One explanation is that we as a people have an inadequate understanding of time. Perhaps we have lost our organic sense of time.

Our world—and you and I within it—has abandoned the traditional notion of cyclical time and replaced it with mechanical time.

As a child, I recall how farmers' lives were guided by the rhythms of nature. The farmers I visited as a child lived by the seasons. They knew when to plant, when to plow and when to harvest. They would peer into the sky, feel the breeze on their face and receive guidance for the next morning.

When I was a student working in a laboratory in Canada's chemical valley, however, no longer did I see the rhythm of the seasons and of dawn and dusk guiding life. Our practices were guided by the clock; factories were operated by employees who worked on shifts: day (8–4), afternoon (4–12) and night (12–8). Such activity in industry and commerce has contributed immensely to the conditions that have diminished the quality of life.

One great lesson available to us today is to ask, "What time is it in the universe?"

The response can be to contemplate the irreversible evolutionary development of time, whose path forward is at the threshold of each new, emergent moment. That moment is not guided by the clock on the wall or watch on the wrist, but by our awareness of deep time. That time before time is simultaneously the instant when the galaxies were born, when life emerged on planet Earth and when the universe gave birth to you and me. As we enter deep time, we become citizens of the universe and are called forth to leave our healing mark on the as-yet-to-be-realized future.

CREATIVITY

Lyrics of the Heart

What is more beautiful
than a poem
sending emanations from the heart,

speaking salutations from on high
about the little things,
both great and small?

Big expectations,
longings of hunger in the heart,
cry out for wisdom not yet known.

So today I write,
this very day I mean,
I write the poem my heart has yet to write.

Is it not an announcement,
an unexpected utterance
spoken from a depths I have yet to know?

Is it not a message,
beyond conscious thought,
about what I have never known or sought to see,

a frail and tender gesture
of all I have to say?
May it always be a gospel of my heart.

Be Alive

Think freely, smile often.
Tell those you love that you do.
Rediscover old friends,
make new ones.

Pick some daisies,
share them.
Keep a promise.
Laugh heartily.

Reach out,
let someone in.
Hug a child.
Slow down.

See a sunrise.
Listen to rain.
Trust life.
Have faith.

Make some mistakes,
learn from them.
Explore the unknown.
Celebrate life.

When the Soul Speaks

Thomas Merton writes, "We have to learn the knack of free association, to let loose what is hidden in our depths, to expand rather than to condense prematurely."

With these words, Merton invites us to dance between custom and nature, discipline and impulse, conscious and unconscious. He invites us to let the soul speak.

I often say that to do this dance, we need to take stock of the many episodes that have defined and shaped our life. These include ecstatic moments as well as painful moments that touched us deeply. These are the destiny signs that shaped our sense of the sacred and brought focus to our days.

And what better way to engage in this process than to write about it. I view writing as a process akin to gathering snow into a huge pile. As we delve into our unconscious and freely associate, we come across all the moments that shaped who we have become. We add each to the pile, and watch the pile grow. We see how each moment, each event, shaped our sense of the sacred. We see the sacred signature of each imprinted on our soul.

Having gone through this gathering process, we are free to take our accumulation of defining episodes and begin to design the contours of a narrative that we wish to unfold. As we design this new story, we punctuate each episode with reflection to clarify the purpose behind our words and thoughts. In this way, we expand and make shareable with the world the deeply personal process that allowed this articulation to happen.

The Doorway of Poetry

Poetry is one doorway to overcome our long addiction to the discursive, the rationalistic, and to do justice to the symbolic and mythopoetic while retrieving an approach to language that is both ecopoetic (nature images) and theopoetic (divine images). Through poetry, we navigate our lives with images, stories and myths.

Poetry evokes responses in the imagination and transports us into another mode of understanding. Through poetry, we let our heart speak. We learn that when life seems clouded and uncertain, perhaps the best thing we can do is write a poem.

Poetry gives expression to the deep interior experience of the soul, where without illusion, we become transparent before the divine indwelling, which activates our soul and summons us to a rich and deeper life.

Welcome Young Poet

Welcome, young poet,
to my new home.

Find a chair on the front porch,
relax and rest.

You are safe here,
enjoy the moment.

Take a sip
of clear, cool water.

Take a ride on the swing
on Aunt Margaret's porch.

Listen to the waves
on the St. Clair shore.

Hear the fog horn
from the freighter on Channel Bank.

Join my mother in the kitchen,
my father on the front porch,
telling stories.

Yes, dear young poet,
you belong here.
You'll always belong here.

Art at the Confluence I

Martha came from Regina,
from Canada's West,
like Trina on her birthday,
a give-away guest.

Yes, she came from the prairie,
from Canada's West,
a companion of magnificence,
born from the confluence
of music and art.

Do you see what I see?
A confluence of all beings
announces its emergence today.

From Quebec, cedar waxwing: present.
From Africa, Nigerian hibiscus: present.
From New Zealand, blue whale: present.
From Australia, kangaroo: present.
From Guam, bird of paradise: present.
From California, sea gull: present.
From Ohio, gecko: present.
From Australia, koala: present.

Each magnificent being
astonishes the soul,
each new companion
makes our world whole.

Art at the Confluence II

Walk among the beings.
Drink gently the sound
of Carolyn's liquid song.

Gather now and imagine
wells of wisdom,
signs of wonderous beauty
born of each soul.

See now with new eyes
what is really here
at the confluence.

Struggle and fulfillment
happen as you see it,
draw it, paint it.

Give an awesome thanks
as you gaze
as the mystery of the cosmos
rises in our midst.

From Trinidad, scarlet iris.
From Antigonish, white swan.
From Australia, Sturt's desert pea.
From Sri Lanka, Asian elephant.
From St. Louis, turtle.
From Japan and Kingston, red dragonfly.
From Youngstown, camellia.
From Ontario, Canadian owl.

Each brings forth wonder.
Each comes forth
to celebrate and beautify Earth.

A Hymn to Creation

Poetry invites us into
the fault lines of our psyches.
We know again the place
where finitude and infinity meet,
where words of mystery
envelop the landscape
that lies deep within.

Poetry washes over us,
as words, however lyrical,
announce once more
that they are the last resort
for what lies deep within.

The new story unfurls before us,
unleashing the divine imagination,
announcing the cosmological powers
that swirl through the universe,
proclaiming with fresh comprehension
humanity's conscious self-awareness.

Peacemaking brings cosmos back to Earth.
With renewed hope,
we feel again the possibility
of a beloved community,
a place where peace can happen always,
where hope becomes our oxygen,
a source of breath,
as we once again inspire each other
and aspire to a healed and healthy Earth.

In this place of energy and zest,
we can grow our soul,
become instruments of promise,
a people of planetary peace,
who know, as if for the first time,
that the universe is constitutive
to all our traditions
and a sacred experience
for openness and life.

Legacy

The urge to leave
something behind,
to pass on to others,
express yourself,
call out to whomever listens:
this is your legacy.

For as long as it takes,
proclaim what you must,
whether anyone listens or not.
Do your work,
do what you must.

Write, paint, sing, proclaim.
Create what is urgent.
Say what you see.
Transform your life.
Befriend the Earth.

New

One more New Year.
New of course,
it never happened before,
not even once.
This moment is entirely new.

It's yours to live
as never before.
Each new moment is
a time to create,
to make life matter.

Each new day is
a precious gift,
to breathe, laugh and play,
as if you never
did before.

In the Zone

The media has been fueled with news about the condition of the knee of Stephan Curry, star of the Golden State Warriors and the most valuable player in the National Basketball Association. Having suffered a sprain, he was out of the lineup for more than two weeks. When he returned this past Monday, his exact role in the game was uncertain. He did not start and instead sat on the bench on a stationary bike, trying to prepare to reenter the game.

When he came onto the court, he missed nine of his first ten shots. But then as the game progressed, something marvelous happened. Steph stepped into the zone. His shots began to fall. When he scored 17 points during overtime to almost singlehandedly win the game, he set an all-time record. He was back!

Michael Murphy and Rhea White wrote a book called *In the Zone*, about the transcendent experience in sports. That book was written twenty years ago, but it could have been about Steph on Monday night. Steph was in the zone. As we watched, his mind, body and spirit coalesced, and he was able to transcend the limits of space and time and lead his team to victory. One after another 3-point shot flew through the hoop. And it all looked so effortless. Congratulations, Warriors!

People gather at sporting events so they can feel part of the community of life. They like competition; they want to see a win. But sometimes it is more than just that. By following the magic of Stephan Curry, each of us is also in some way inspired to do more than we might otherwise do, to transcend what we might think we are. To become planetary people who live in the zone.

Imaginings

May you be seized by a dream,
be passionate about what lies
beyond conscious thought.

May your imagination soar,
your vision be a portal to new life.

Now is the time for aliveness,
to make the story matter
and the future real.

Now is the time to hope,
pray and struggle
at the doorway of a new tomorrow.

Meander through the lessons
of yesterday and bid the past goodbye.

Celebrate the divine nudges that bring hope.
Set your imagination free:
this is why you are here.

At the Edge

It is here that life happens,
here at the edge of sadness,
at the interface of gratitude and grief.
It is here that we feel the impact
of an emergent force
rising from within.

Emergence

Let every surge,
every possibility,
every burst of energy
emerge into the light of day.

Let every silent sound
heal the heart
and bring belonging
to the world.

The Call to Live

There's a pulse in my soul
that wants to live,
a song to be sung,
a melody that matters.

I feel an inclination
to restore and resacralize the world,
that all may be hopeful,
that all may be free.

A Pilgrimage to the Divine in and Though Creation

The Christian life is often mysterious and full of questions as we journey forward. Today we gather in community without knowing what lies ahead. We look into the future and stutter in amazement as we discover ourselves surrounded by new companions, new teachers, a new landscape and new friends.

Is this not an opportunity to ponder over our lives and breathe deeply into the still, soft atmosphere of forgiveness and compassion that is rising into awareness? At the same time, we feel the conviction that it is still possible to stop, turn around and begin again.

This is a time to reflect, heal, forgive and look forward. May pain dissolve into forgiveness. May judgment and oppression dissolve into the embrace of fresh energy. May gratitude liberate us from the burdens of the past. May blame dissolve and gently float away.

Another way to become transported into a new awareness is to ask what courage and trust it would take to experience your journey and your life as entirely new. Ask how the opportunity for solitude and companionship influences you as you walk upon the land and among the trees, and refresh your body and irrigate your soul.

As you embark on this quest for new life, set aside some silent moments to reflect on the signs of our time and silently encourage the sacred impulses that are bubbling into awareness and inviting you to respond. This time of rest is refreshment for the days ahead. It is the foundation for your great work.

The Sabbath is a precious time when you are called to let go of preoccupations and deepen your awareness. Immerse yourself in the scripture of your life and engage in the lectio divina of your spiritual journey through a threefold process:

1. Through story, reflect on the narrative of your family, the land where they settled, the stories they told, the values they lived by and the livelihood with which they lived and nurtured their young.

2. Select a passage from scripture or a gospel story that speaks to you, and explore its significance in images, memories and myths that speak to you today.

3. With pen and paper, spend a period of solitary reflection and compose and name the sacred impulses that hover in your awareness. Identify actions you hope to pursue in the days that follow.

When you then return to the world of engagement, your participation will bring a keener awareness of the joys and sorrows of the people and of the planet at this time in human/Earth history.

We can agree with the columnist who characterized the tenor of our current political and social culture by saying, "A faith that makes losing a sin will make cheating a sacrament."

We live in a noisy world in which we are constantly affected by—and even become addicted to—television and computers and smart phones. During these days, we are challenged to become more and more deeply aware of the divine presence in our midst.

Throughout history, as we moved from an oral culture to a print culture and now to a digital culture, the need for spiritual breakthrough has become increasingly important. Through community building, we are able to retrieve a sense of oral history and enjoy meaningful conversations that can dissolve the separateness of electronic media. Only then are we able to speak about and test our insights.

When Thomas Merton welcomed Ernesto Cardenal, he saw both a poet and a politician, someone who was imaginative and intuitive, and could speak and write from the center of his sacredness and also use his thoughts to influence the context of everyday existence. Yes, we can agree that each of us is now being called to be both a poet and a politician.

With the reality that we live in a patriarchal culture, women are too frequently treated as "less than." Yet when they let their souls speak, they may reveal that they are close to the divine and have access to another mode of understanding than that of the dominant male culture. Misogynistically, men sometime view this negatively or understand women as a danger. I suggest that the only way to heal the wounds of fear is to form a more mutually enhancing relationship.

With this in mind, we take up the challenge as people of faith to be the deepest and most authentic we can. We hold the belief that Christ is truly risen and his enveloping cosmic presence is alive among us.

To establish a deep and authentic interior that will guide us into the future, we look to the symbols, images and vision that offer fresh approaches that are imaginative, lyrical and spontaneous. The pilgrim's journey opens us to the embrace of beauty and into a nourishing flow of awe and wonder.

As we become enveloped in the upstart spring of natural grace, which reveals we are all immersed in the presence of the divine creative energy that resides at the intersection of humanity and God, life takes on a sacramental nature. Like melody and song, the interior life becomes the energetic source that is liberating and promises a flourishing and vibrant world.

Alive

There are words in me
I wish to tell the world.
Hope has put a pen
in my hand.

Tomorrow will come.
The sun will rise.
The child will grow.
Celebrate each moment.

Rise with delight.
Question what is possible.
Say thanks daily
to the challenges life presents.

NATURE

Great River

This river, such beauty;
this river, so wide.
The river before me
would be my bride.

She healed me,
she held me when I was in pain.
She carried me,
she cared for me
when I swam and I played.

St. Clair, I thank you.
Flow on, dear river.
Blue stream of beauty,
ripples of wisdom,
my healer, my friend,
St. Clair, I love you.

Healing Power of Grace

Even from miles away,
the St. Clair seems so close.
Its memories trickle in my mouth
as I fast approach
the poultice of my heart,
where these memories reside.
In my child's cosmic home,
I swim, skate, fish.
I discover once again
the healing power of grace.

Voices

Voices call out to me.
I hear the wolf cry.
The breeze renders its gentle call.

God is everywhere—
in the deep blue, azure sky,
in the high eucalyptus
standing stately on the cliff.

There is a chorus of voices
in our midst,
echoing from the recesses of our souls
and rising from the deep, dark ground of life.

On Signal Hill

Where are You,
God of Cabot tower and rock,
sacred home of moose, trees and struggle?

Perhaps You are in the snowdrifts
washing on the Stephenville shore
or the panoramic view from Signal Hill.

Or are You the cabin resting on high,
overlooking a breathless vision
of Your great Earth?

Theater of Love

Birds proclaim their a cappella song.
A spider weaves its web.
Children celebrate
ring around the rosy.
Even the frog on the riverbank
jumps for joy.

Is not the world around you
a theater of love?
It is God's new creation.
You are invited to
play your part,
sing your song.

Quest

A question came from the far-off sky:
will you live in the live oak forest forever?
To this, I answered no.
It is not in my plans.

Rather, I am here for now,
to listen to the trees, the rain, the land;
to become attentive
to the sunshine and clouds;
to listen to the wordless wisdom
from on high
and on Earth below.

This is my quest for peace
in this torn and tattered world.

Rose

I want to live like a rose,
without agendas or regrets.
I hear hidden voices say,
"Break the chains of conformity."
See the lilies in the field,
the cattle as they graze.
Listen my friend,
let the Earth teach you.
Heed the compass of your heart.

Solitude and Silence

Listen, listen, hear Earth speak.
Hear the whisper from a hidden,
unknown God.

Tales of self-discovery
are a journey of the heart.
Stories of salvation
tell of a healing Earth.

I pray these silent thoughts today,
glad for the solitude of the forest.

Solitude and Song

Another day in the low country.
The fields are quiet.
The solitude of the forest
stirs my heart.

From this nourishing
well of silence, once again,
out of apparent nothingness,
the bell of freedom rings.

From the shores of California
to the lowlands of South Carolina,
out of silence and stillness,
freedom songs are born.

Every Tree that Falls

I believe in every tree that falls,
every person who dreams,
every voice echoing from the depths,
every impulse of my heart.

Bathe us in the beauty of this day.
Sanctify and bless his transitional moment.

From the depths of all that is,
recognize the sacred
in every tree that falls
and leaves an imprint on your soul.

Colors

"Color me yellow," you say.
I say, "Color me blue."

Wash my heart in the velvet sky.
Soak my soul in azure blue.

Plunge me into an ocean of teal.
Rest my soul on a pillow of blue.

Remind me also of the bright red sun.
Dream deeply of fire and rain.

Allow the sparks of sunshine
to flow into my soul.

"De colores," I hear creation say.
So it is. May all colors be.

St. Francis Day

Sanctified in truth,
I hear St. Francis say,
"Feed the hungry, heal the wounded."
Send out joyful hymns of praise
to all our cousins of creation.
Offer prayers of adoration
across the land, sea and sky.
Remember, you are truly blessed
on this St. Francis Day.

A Canine Conversation

Good morning, Shelly.
Tell me about your paw,
the left one injured in the field.
Is it better now?

Tell me, Shelly,
how are you today?
What did you dream about
last night, when after kibble,
you yawned and stretched,
then slept long into the night.

Tell me, Shelly,
are you happy
here at the Hermitage,
the place among
the oak and cedar forests
we call home?

Tell me, Shelly,
do you like the sunshine
on the back porch?
Quiet dinners on the rug?
Are you happy here
as you frolic in the fields
and palmetto sun?

Geography of God

There are many
revelations
here on Earth.

Bras d'Or Lake in Nova Scotia,
meaning golden arm,
but pronounced
like my mother's name.

Trinidad is the island
of the three mountains,
the land of the trinity,
indeed a sacred place.

I give great thanks
to the geography of God,
to each and every place
where you and God can dwell.

~BEAUTY~

Beauty: The Work of the Creator

The indigenous mind sees the divine in many manifestations. Each unique expression—be it a rock, water or tree—is beautiful in God's sight.

Some years ago, I participated in a program whose focus was justice and the cosmos. There, I discovered another name for justice; that name is *beauty*. When I later reflected on the universe and the Earth, I realized that they flow out of the divine imagination and bathe us all in a shimmering cloak of beauty.

Beauty also flows into our lives through the song of a robin, the gurgle of a brook and the gift of music. We receive beauty, for instance, through the melodious response of Paul Winter, who with his alto clarinet echoes the sounds of the forest. We likewise receive it through the songs of the wolf, the elephant and the eagle.

Beauty reveals itself to us when we ponder deeply as the mystery of mathematics flows into our soul through the amazing harmony of numbers, symbols and sound.

Beauty is available to us in each sacred moment when we gather as friends of God and prophets to create together the conditions in which beauty can shine forth.

Today it suddenly came to me that we have received the gift of beauty from our ancestors, the First Nation's people and all God's creatures who preceded us on planet Earth. As they walked, flew, swam, built homes and cared for their young, each brought his or her gift of beauty to this land.

During these days at Springbank, we become more and more aware that we also are living on this land to bring forth beauty into the world.

Philosopher and poet John O'Donohue writes, "The beautiful stirs passion and urgency in us.... It unites us again with the neglected and forgotten grandeur of life." As I contemplate his words, I arrive at the awareness that each expression is itself beautiful in its own way.

I am thrilled to announce once again to the world that "Black is beautiful." And I also wish to add, "so are Red, Brown, Yellow, and White."

As we gain an enhanced appreciation of beauty, it becomes clear that it is revealed to us in very different ways. When the celebrant at Bernstein's Mass dropped the crystal chalice on the terrazzo floor, he gazed at the glistening crystals and at all who gathered in the cathedral that amazing day, and proclaimed, "I never thought that brokenness could be so beautiful."

Beauty is indeed a mystery and a great gift; we can say with confidence that beauty happens when we discover that we are truly ourselves and allow our gifts to shine through. The same is true of the oak tree, the vegetables in Sr. Barbara's garden, the luscious food prepared at Sr. Mary Dean's table, the taiji we practice in the morning with Sr. Trina, the healing oils of Sr. Theresa as they activate the vibrational energy and the healing presence of Marcia on the land as she gives her gift to beautify this plantation place.

In and through the memories of each indigenous mind, we reactivate the ancestral grace of those who have gone on before and who today activate our memories of a world of beauty, wonder and belonging.

This morning as I gazed out the eastern window to welcome the morning sun, I experienced a felt sense of the divine as beauty adorning the forest and the fields below. I felt their beauty flow gently upon my heart and soul.

As I contemplate that moment, I ask, "Is not our gift to the world our capacity to create the conditions for beauty to shine forth?"

At Swan Lake

At Swan Lake,
creatures of divinity sail by,
paddling across velvet waters.
They greet all who wander
the shores of their tranquil lake.

Stately swans,
some white, some black,
glide and fly,
then gently come to rest,
on this Swan Lake afternoon.

A Basket of Beauty

There is a rhythm in the weave:
weave fold weave,
weave fold weave,
red beige blue,
weave fold weave.

A basket of memories,
a tapestry of time
where stories are told,
friendships formed,
imaginations released,
memories tucked safely away.

From it all will emerge
a basket of beauty:
provisions for the journey
for the hungry, lonely and lost,
bread for the world.

All Is Beauty

I hear wind.
I feel rain.
I see dark nights
and bright days.

Enthusiastic moments
follow doorways to despair.
I envision triumph,
ponder loss.

All is beauty now.
Yes, all is beauty.

Even in the wind and rain,
darkness and light,
triumph and loss,
even in divisions,
all is beauty now.
All is beauty.

We Grow our Soul

To experience the beauty of creation is to have a sacramental consciousness by which we recognize the face of God in all of nature. This is another kind of literacy that all of us are capable of, but sometimes not conscious of, when we read God's face in a sunrise or sunset, a bluebonnet flower, a storm, a mountain range, a prairie, an ocean. These are the moments when creation speaks to us and tells us the story of the universe.

David Steindl-Rast, the great Benedictine of our time, says, "Beauty seen makes the one who sees it more beautiful." And Jim Couture, a graduate of the Sophia Center program, wrote, "The cavity of our souls needs to be filled with the wonder and awe of the natural world." We grow our soul every time we respond to such beauty.

A Smokey Mountain Whisper

Over there,
in the Smokey Mountain mist,
birds fly low,
motorcycles and trucks pass by.
Over there,
the Smokey Mountains' beauty
activates your soul.

Trees in pastel hues
of red, yellow and green
dance into our awareness,
as if a divine artist
has adorned the azure sky
with lavish strokes of wonder,
while the Blue Ridge Mountains
whisper words of wisdom
to my heart.

Each New Tomorrow

"Cheer up! Cheer up!"
I hear the children say.
You are not alone.

Be not afraid.
You are loved
by the puppy, live oak and rain.

Life is brief,
yet O so beautiful.
Be here now.

Quench your thirst for solitude.
Make communion with trees.
Let beauty heal your soul.

Now, and each new tomorrow.

Make Us One

Imagine a world
with a beatific eye,
new moments
of grateful recollections
and abundant beauty.

Beauty dissolves
dangerous memories
that bring to mind
all that for which
today I pray.

Shower me with mercy,
cleanse, purify and protect
the fragile and endangered ones
who call out to all creation,
"Make us one again,
make us one again!"

A Portal to Beauty

New portals appear, as doorways open. One moment marks a closing and ignites one more new beginning.

When we approach a threshold, feeling we have given all and are at the conclusion of a journey, something new happens. Although we're empty, there is the beginning of something new.

Moments of intuition begin to stir within. From the depth of things still unexpressed, a canticle is born. A soul song radiates from the wellsprings of our soul.

Embedded within the human psyche is a relentless desire to flourish, an aspiration that calls us to reach out for the unreachable and take action toward the good.

Within this desire is the profound conviction about our original goodness. We desire a time when life is more beautiful, and all creation is seen as a sacred place where beauty shines through.

I Wonder

A great baldheaded eagle
hovers over Earth,
soaring across
the landscape of the north.
From within
the many questions of my heart,
I discover a depth of beauty
I have never known.
At the doorway of surprises,
I listen to our silent God.

Song of Beauty

What is more ordinary
than prayer?

Each moment
inaugurates a breath,
the inhalation and exhalation
of existence.

Each moment
an invitation
to pay attention
to the wordless silence
of the Earth.

Each moment
a choir of adoration,
a song of beauty.

The frog plays bass,
the cricket tenor—
Earth's symphony of beauty.

MYSTERY

God of Countless Mystery

God of mystery,
source of love and life,
You reveal Yourself to us
in so many countless ways.
From the vast and endless cosmos
to the monstrance of every beating heart,
we send a joyful song of praise,
and as a people, we all say,
"Thank You, thank You and Amen!"

Cosmos and Soul

Soul searchers, gentle people—
each one made a fierce commitment
to society and soul.
These are people of trust,
friends of Earth, art and spirit,
sources of friendship,
companions of hope.

We gather this Monday
in a stellar moment
when the sun rests gently
into the disappearing sky,
accompanied by the waning moon,
whose lunar face
recedes into the far-off sky.

At this defining time,
a time beyond all times,
a darkness only God could know
settles across the opaque dimensions.
We plunge into our searching souls,
peer into the sacred heart of God,
to discover there a nascent illuminating night.

Incarnational Moments

For me, the incarnation is not just an event that happened two thousand years ago, as it certainly did. It is the ongoing outburst of life that we see when the sun comes up in the morning, when a flower blooms, when a child is born, when an idea emerges in our imagination or when instinct or impulse calls people together. These are all incarnational moments, a time in which the living God is made visible among us.

With this perspective, the cross can be understood beyond the historical Good Friday. Within the cosmic crucifixion reside the Gethsemane moments of a wasted life, of enduring poverty, of depleted resources, of an extractive economy, of a politics ruled by greed and special interests, of a despair that permeates the soul of our youth, of the hunger for meaning that resides within all hearts.

So too the resurrection, our Easter, becomes an ongoing event. It happens when we become one with our God, with our loved ones, and with our Earth. It happens through moments of surprise, in times of prayer when we move from illusion to reality. We realize that prayer is not as much about petition or contrition as about celebration and praise, about aligning ourselves with the unfolding of life, rather than asking God to make the world the way we would like it to be. We make our Easter with the Earth not just at the spring equinox but when our lives and our gatherings create an experience of communion that is alive and full.

Door of the Unexpected

Who is that knocking,
knocking on my door,
the door of the unexpected?

Anger, fear, hope, love
and everything in between,
between the hopes and fears
of these so many years
that today are still alive,
alive to wonder, courage and gratitude,
alive to life at this very moment.

Drink deeply of yesterday now,
and also of tomorrow,
a tomorrow that may never come,
that may never come.

Emptiness

Who are you, emptiness?
What do you want?

Are you a friend
or perhaps a foe?

Tell me about what you mean
when you speak of an invitation
to come closer to God.

O yes, dear emptiness,
I see that you yourself
are the mystery.

Now I hear you, empty one.
Invite me in.

Let me come closer to the loved one,
to God.

Love

Love is a mystery,
a magnetic intuition.
It begins with God
and activates our hearts.

It is a cosmic response,
an invitation
to fall into
the divine embrace.

Love is a response
to Jesus of the cosmos and the cross,
who shines forth
in every blade of grass
and every moment
we dare to call our life.

Just for a Minute

There is a place of wonder,
a place that is holy, mysterious
and sometimes hidden.
A place I've longed for all my life,
a place to visit, embrace, plunge into.
A deep place
where I as of yet have never been.
A place where I long to linger,
to activate something
for which I have no words.
A place to discover and dream,
where just for a minute
I know what purpose
and meaning could be.

Only God Could Know

They come, they go.
They come, they go,
go to far-off places.

Australia, New Zealand,
Guam and Montreal,
California and Ohio.

They come, and then they go
to a place of wonder,
welcome and surprise.

From this place, their place
of wonder and belonging,
they begin again.

Indeed, they begin again
to create a feeling
only God could know.

Salutations

In the midst of uncertainty,
I stop to listen,
maybe even pray.

"Let go," I hear the prophets call,
"join the cosmic dance."

There is so much to ponder,
so many questions to ask.

Take up the banner.
Salute the unknown.
Behind the shroud of uncertainty
resides your illuminated path.

Gazing into Mystery

How do I tell you
about mystery,
share with you
those precious things
I still do not know?

The chickadee could tell you,
"I'm confident,"
as could the raven and the cat.

It's my words
that get in the way.
My soul knows
what as yet I cannot tell.

Gaze into the mystery.
Let your questions say it all.

~HOPE~

Ripples of Hope

Throughout my life, I have been confronted with issues and disappointments that crushed my spirit and dashed my hopes.

I reflect now on the last year in the life of Thomas Merton, who died in December 1968. That spring, Dr. Martin Luther King, Jr. was felled by an assassin's bullet as he stood on the porch of a Memphis hotel. The same evening, Robert F. Kennedy gave the most moving eulogy I've ever heard as he announced to the people the news of Martin's death.

As Kennedy spoke, an unforeseen tragic irony was about to take place. He himself was killed two months later, in a hotel in Los Angeles, as he campaigned for the nomination of the Democratic Party.

Now we reflect on the challenges of our day, as we move forward from election day November 8, 2016. At this defining moment for the world, we ponder the results of the vote. We watch as the echoes reverberate around the country, and indeed around the world. It seems that the mood of the people has changed—in one way or the other.

We pray that our country rises to a better day, infused with the hope and trust of those who join us on the way. Each time a person stands up for an ideal or seeks to improve the lot of others or strikes out against injustice, he or she sends forth a tiny ripple of hope. And that ripple, combined with a myriad others, can sweep down even the mightiest walls of oppression and injustice.

A Marvelous Gift

Hope is a marvelous gift,
like a sparrow in flight,
a pickerel in the pond,
a child in the meadow.

We embrace each moment,
transcend despair.
We hope for a better tomorrow,
joyful children,
sunshine and winter,
ponies in the field,
blackbirds in the sky,
hearts alive,
visions clear.

Tomorrow's promise is here:
hope is a marvelous gift.

Stirred

From our cool winter slumber,
we welcome,
sometimes reluctantly,
a splash of illumination,
as Earth awakes.

I am stirred to say,
"Now is the time
to make a new beginning,"
as the hills and oceans say,
"Trust our wisdom."

Follow the sun.
Vote with your feet.
Welcome tomorrow.
At the break of dawn,
one more day.

Meant to Be

There is hope
in my heart,
a pulsating passion,
an enduring echo of aliveness,
that incessantly knocks on the door
of each new tomorrow.

This hope is
an arrow to the future;
it penetrates the cloud of unknowing,
soars to the pinnacle of aliveness,
presides at the turning point
of each new tomorrow.

This hope is
an incessant invitation
to rest and reside
where we are and
where we were always
meant to be.

Cleanse

Now is the time.
Let the unimagined happen,
fulfill what is unexpected.
Let the new
cleanse your soul.
Arise, my friends;
celebrate another day.

Arise, my friends;
recover hope.
Cast off all tendencies
of apathy, mistrust.
Celebrate a dream
that heals all separation.
Rise up, my friends;
heal the hearts
of all who try to take us down.

Promise and Possibility

The sun peeks out
from among the shadows
of a disappearing night.
It seems that
out of nowhere
another day is born.

With courage, gratitude, and wisdom,
we compose a new chapter
of an as-yet-unfolding story.
It is a story of power,
open to the possibility
of a new day.

It will be a day of promise,
a day that embodies
the vitality of hope and celebration.
This vision will energize our efforts,
bring healing to the planet
and its people.

Opening

Remain open,
open to the world,
open to tomorrow,
open to surprise.

Realize the possibility.
Tomorrow awaits.
Prepare the way.
Let tomorrow in.

Shouting Back

Today I stand up to face the world,
a world lacerated by wounds
of race, dollars and psychic pain.

In the midst of so much sorrow,
I search for and discover a hope
that springs from the heart of Earth,
from buried seeds that refuse to die,
a resurrection of new life.

Hope comes from the center of things,
where all that remains unexpressed
surges to the surface and shouts,
"Here I am. Listen to me!"

Today I shout at the universe
and wait for the universe to shout back.

Emptiness and Rest

Roll back, roll back,
roll back the stone,
the stone of despair.

Break open, break open
the tomb of emptiness and hope,
from which all newness flows.
Satiate all longing,
be at home and rest.

The Promise

Sometimes wisdom lies lifeless
in the tomb of life's unconscious,
wriggling, swirling, struggling
for breath, for freedom
and the capacity to see what is hidden,
reveal what is true.

Yet somewhere in wells
of uncertainty and doubt,
where the shadow of opaqueness
blurs our vision,
a trickle of clarity
bubbles up from within.

Only then
will the cosmos and the soul
flow together
and nurture the promise of new life.

Another Spark

In the center of my being,
a heartbeat, a pulse of life,
awakening each artery of existence.

Welcoming the emergence of new life,
even within the shadows and darkness,
I feel a spark of hope.

The Divine Drama in Everyday Experience

The good news of the gospel has been made available to the believing community through a variety of worldviews over time.

A metaphor for these shifting worldviews can be found in the science of optics. When a beam of light is focused on a glass crystal, it is refracted into a variety of colors and wavelengths. Even so, each beam retains the original qualities of the light. Similarly, when the good news of the gospel is made available to the Christian community through different worldviews, the people of God are nonetheless able to receive the same original divine revelation.

When the early church was influenced by the cosmology of Plato, that Christian story was made available to the people. During those early years, St. Augustine composed his major work, *The City of God*. In the middle ages, Thomas Aquinas was invited to Rome when the cosmology of Aristotle began to influence the worldview of the West. Aquinas composed his most significant work through writing the *Summa Theologica*. These theological reflections remain foundational to the Christian world even today.

We live in a time when a new worldview is emerging into human consciousness. We are now invited to experience the good news of the gospel through evolutionary eyes. The new cosmic story was pioneered by paleontologist and theologian Pierre Teilhard de Chardin and cultural historian and geologian Thomas Berry. Teilhard's *The Human Phenomenon* and Berry's *The Dream of the Earth*, *The Great Work*, and *The Universe Story* (with Brian Swimme) stand as a powerful response to religious alienation and ecological devastation.

The good news of the gospel becomes available to us in a variety of ways, including through the receptivity of our soul and the cultural context in which we live.

When our psyche is open to receiving the good news, we are able to cheerfully receive it in amazing ways, as our sense of the divine comes flowing into our experience through everything we see, feel, touch, smell and taste. Through openness and anticipation, we drink in the shimmering beauty of an azure river, the stately power of a tree and the awesome wonder of a bird's flight in the far-off sky.

As our hearts open, they are filled with an enduring hope that tomorrow will transcend our fondest aspirations and be even more beautiful than today. As we engage in dialogue with friends, we enjoy companionship and are moved to embrace the dawn of a new tomorrow.

The gospel comes to us through the lens of each cultural moment in which we live, move and experience life. We view God not as a supreme being extrinsic to human life but rather as an enveloping divine presence in our life. As each of us courageously engages the forces that hold us back, we receive the liberating power of the spirit that transforms any illusion of difference between the sacred and the secular. As we move forward into our lives, we experience an enhanced capacity for love and for work and the ability to bare frustration. We experience an infusion of grace that empowers us to cheerfully respond to the needs of the world.

As believing people, we are newly aware that the good news of the gospel is available to us in and through the images and stories we tell, as expressed through the joys and sorrows of the people we are privileged to serve.

In these moments of engagement and reflection, we become empowered to continually restore and reinvigorate the forms and structures of creation, lest they regress and begin to oppose their original purpose. The process of engagement in personal and social transformation, empowered by the holy spirit, is available to us through dialogue, information and support.

In different regions of the planet, people live out the call of the gospel in their particular context. Among these contexts is liberation theology in South and Central America, in response to the poverty and unjust distribution of the Earth's resources. The prophetic voice of Gustavo Gutierrez, as announced in A Theology of Liberation, expressed a powerful response to the meaning of the gospel in this context. A response to apartheid in South Africa became the womb of contextual theology, as articulated by Albert Nolan in dialogue with Desmond Tutu, Nelson Mandela and others. In Canada, Gregory Baum wrote about critical theology as a first-world application of liberation theology.

James Cone wrote on Black theology, addressing the Black experience in America. Rosemary Radford Ruether wrote on ecofeminist theology, addressing the oppression of women and Earth in *Gaia and God*. Elizabeth Johnston's *Quest for the Living God* is an epic work that names the theologies that have arisen to awaken hearts and minds at this defining moment in human/Earth history.

Resolving the Divide

Prompted by the movement of the spirit, we awaken to the great adventure that awaits us. We anticipate a vigorous infusion of divine creative energy to transform mind, body and soul. With Elizabeth Johnson, we envision "a flourishing humanity, on a thriving planet rich in species in an evolving universe, all together filled with the glory of God."

The hoped-for result will be a deepening experience of divine presence that holds all things in one numinous embrace. As we are transported by this new cosmic vision of beauty, wonder and belonging, we will discover more than we could have imagined. No longer confined by static dogma, we will enjoy the dynamic integration of our religious inheritance with evolutionary science. We will be called forward into the unfinished and ever-changing moment that we embrace as the omega point.

A central problem is that we have failed to bridge the distance between religion and our experience in the world. Creating this bridge was the primary motivation of Thomas Berry and Teilhard de Chardin. They lived at a time when theology saw the spiritual works of mercy as infused with supernatural grace, while social justice (the corporal works of mercy) was relegated to an inferior place infused with natural grace. The result was the failure of religion to meet the needs of the people.

Humanity's challenge is to resolve the divide of two faiths: faith in God and faith the world. For too long, we have viewed the love of God as a gift of sanctifying grace, and have viewed the love of Earth and the work of justice making as a result of natural grace. Today, our evolutionary faith dissolves any distinction between our love of God and love of the world, as we anticipate a future culminating in the embrace of the omega point that is manifest in the cosmic Christ, whereby every molecule of existence is soaked in the divine creative power of the triune God.

Our Fondest Hope

This is in fact
our place,
our future,
our fondest hope.

Our aspirations
reside somewhere
in far-off mystery,
where wisdom dwells,
within the recesses of our souls.

After the Storm

A serene autumn day
in Williamsburg County,
water flows,
a warm, cleansing shower
refreshes body and soul.

"When will light return?"
I ask from Magnolia Porch.
"Hopefully tomorrow,"
an echo answers back.
Yes! Hopefully tomorrow.

Risen

Whether in despair or wonder,
the sun will rise tomorrow,
day will follow night.

When the road ahead lies hidden,
an inner light will illuminate
opaqueness in your soul.

The future holds promise
for a risen tomorrow.

~MERCY~

Friend of Prophets

Friend of God and prophets,
source of love and life,
we honor your wisdom
and your words.

Listen with the ear of your heart.
Cultivate the garden of the soul,
that deep interior place
where mercy dwells.

Draw ever closer
to where fresh water flows,
where delight happens,
and the castles of creation dwell.

The Closing of the Prison Door

This incident, which was told to me by an Irish official, occurred when the inmates of Mount Joy Women's Prison in Dublin, Ireland, were being transferred to a new facility. It was Christmas Eve, and an older female prisoner stepped forward and declared to the man in charge, "I want to be the one to close the door for the last time!"

When he asked why, she declared, "I have the right. My grandmother was here, my mother was here, my sisters were here, my baby sister was born here, and I'm here!"

Following her plea, she was selected to close the door for the last time.

At the new prison, after the liturgy on Christmas Day, she clung to a photo of her closing the door, and walked around showing it to everyone present. It was a sad yet poignant moment. On the day that we remember the birth of the liberating Christ, she was proud she had been selected to close the door to the prison that had housed the women of her family over so many years.

Her story reminds us of our need to be chosen, to be recognized, to have our value acknowledged. She challenges us to cultivate a willingness to listen with our hearts, to accept the humanity of the other—her value, experience, wisdom, pain and unrealized potential. Prisoners are often looked upon as dangerous and damaged, as people without status, esteem or respectability. With the eye of mercy, we realize that each of us in our way is doing time, each of us is imprisoned in the cellblock of internalized oppression, the iron cage of the system that lives within.

Ambassadors of Mercy

With courage and confidence,
we respond with renewed hope
to the challenges before us.
We say a resounding yes.

May we embrace
a preferential choice,
become ambassadors of mercy
to the forgotten and left behind.

Venture forth.
Awaken hope and joy.
May all our companions
be healed of isolation, suffering and pain.

Lesson

I'm afraid, Lord.
The days and years go by,
signs of aging are everywhere.
Friends pass on,
colleagues are in pain.
The days are numbered for us all.
This lesson I must learn:
teach me now how to live
and how to die.

The Mercy of Your Heart

Source of all mercy,
bless the marginal ones,
those who hover
on the outside
looking in.

Send forth, O Welcoming One,
an invitation to belong.
Embrace us now.
Bring us closer
to Your heart.

The Practice of Compassion

Compassion is being in an equal relationship with those in need, whether human or other-than-human. Compassion is not doing something for someone to make him or her feel inferior. Meister Eckhart says, "The soul is where God works compassion." We grow our soul by the practice of compassion.

Eckhart also says the best name for God is compassion. My image of compassion is that of a mother embracing her child, holding her close while being willing to let go when the time comes. This reminds me of the divine embrace of the universe, which I see as a curvature of compassion. We live in the arms of a universe where there is a balance between the forces of expansion and gravity. If either element were out of balance, our universe would not exist. The point of harmony is an expression of the curvature of compassion.

This key reality of our universe—that our life depends on achieving equilibrium—is reflected in many aspects of human life, such as our striving to balance our need for both continuity and discontinuity, or innovation and tradition, in healthy ways. We need continuity with our roots, but we also need to live in this moment, making the tradition present and palpable today. Reflecting on the image of the divine curvature of compassion will give us insight, strength and compassion as we work to change the structures and worldview that have become desacralized.

Arc of Compassion

Wisdom flourishes and abounds.
Squirrel dances from limb to limb,
stops to look,
then darts away.
Blackbirds hover in the sky,
surveying all of us below.

Puppies, birds, kittens
take their place in church,
although already blessed
on this Saint Francis Day,
when all of life
is gift, grace and promise.

Even the asphalt jungle,
of this city is a chapel
where homeless saints abide.
All is holy now,
nothing lies outside
the compassionate embrace
of the wise and Ancient One.

Inspiration

Breathe new life today,
that abundant love
may inspire
a little piece of God.

Transform all who behold
this fragile world,
with waves of mercy,
salutations of rapture.

Bring forgiveness
to those who long for mercy,
that they may be inspired
to heal our broken world.

An MRI of the Soul

One year ago,
a young White man
knelt and prayed with nine Black people,
then shot all nine and took their lives.
What might be revealed by an MRI of his soul?

Just days ago,
a man stepped into an Orlando club,
began to shoot.
Forty-nine lost their lives,
others were wounded.
What would be revealed by an MRI of his soul?

Today we ask,
"How is peace possible when love is denied?"
The Golden Rule is not kept
when terror rules the soul.
Perhaps we need
another Selma moment for the soul.

Be with Us Now

Praise be to You,
source of compassion,
friend of the outcast
and all cast aside.

Be with us today,
at this endangered time,
when the poor are hungry,
and Earth awash in wanton waste.

Be with us now.
Heal our broken world.
Mend our anxious hearts.
Pour upon us rivers of hope.

Listen to our call for mercy.
Be with us now.

~GRATITUDE~

Deo Gracias

There is so much to be grateful for.
We say Deo gracias
to the stars twinkling in the night,
for a loved one who has escaped death's grip,
for the sunshine that gracefully greets each morning.

There is a thanksgiving time in every day.
Sun breaks through and arrives again.
When night appears,
we say our prayers,
grateful for another day.

Weekly Report

We look back
at the days gone by.
With hope and trust,
we anticipate the days ahead.

As people of faith,
we give thanks to our God.

Our society is overwhelmed
by gun violence
and the destruction of Earth.

We draw closer each night
and embrace our children
as they go off to sleep

In a special way,
we tell those we love
that we do.

We cherish the words of Pope Francis,
who encourages us to serve
the poor, hungry and lonely,
while protecting God's good Earth.

We gather this morning,
grateful for one new beginning,
listen once again to the sacred scriptures
read aloud to us today.

We give thanks
to our good and gracious God,
like a mother who holds her
newborn child to her breast.

We gaze at Jesus of the cosmos and cross,
our hearts moved by the wonder of it all.
We break open the gospel story,
ponder its meaning for today.

As Christian people,
we remember our origins,
give thanks for the great gift of faith.

We come to the altar to receive the risen Christ,
confident this food for the journey
will provide courage and wisdom
for the days ahead.

Grateful Admiration

Jesus of the Earth and all creation,
let us join in partnership with you.
Bring joy to the world,
hope to all creation,
and grateful admiration
to each pulsating fabric,
as a manifestation of cosmic love.

Soul Ajar

Keep your heart open.
Hold your soul ajar.
Be grateful for each new day.
Welcome the sunrise.
Say goodbye each evening
with gratitude and praise.

Thanks

I hear Earth speak
silent words of grace,
appreciation and praise.

The sun tells tales of radiance,
filtered through maple and oak,
bathes the rocks and earth below.

Long before
Jesus of the cosmos and cross appeared,
You gave birth to Your dream:
gardens of beauty,
our sacred home,
Mother Earth.

Blessed be,
this place of beauty,
gratitude and praise.

Memories

Memories of days long past
take on a fresh and present look.
Time collapses,
the future becomes an ever-present now.
Yesterday becomes tomorrow.

Now is the time, my friend.
Embrace yesterday.
Celebrate today.
Welcome tomorrow.

I give thanks for all that ever was:
the Saint Clair River,
the great Canadian maple,
the yards and ball fields
where we played,
the church we attended,
the two-room schoolhouse
where we studied.

I am home now.
Blessed be.
Yes, blessed be.

Canadian Night Owl

Canadian night owl,
offspring of Ontario ancestral grace,
being of wisdom,
child of river and of earth,
source of all guidance,
shining in the darkness
on this autumn moonlit night,
here at the confluence.
We give great thanks
to our wise and friendly friend.

Carolina Morning

Air crisp,
trees tall,
sun up,
Shelly the dog
prances in the field
on this Carolina morning.

Thank you,
Invisible One,
for this new day
to walk upon
Your canvas of beauty
with delight,
breathe fresh, cool air,
whisper words of gratitude
for the beauty of Your art.

Another Day

The sun rises slowly
over the palmetto state,
turning the dark and serene
into radiance.

Bailey the dog
yawns, stretches, looks around,
then choosing a better fate,
goes back to sleep.

Another day arrives
with gratitude and grace.
We again give thanks
and celebrate the wonder of it all.

Crossroads

With the gift of years,
we take a look back
at what has gone before.

A meaningful life involves
simple satisfaction with one's place
and the promise of another tomorrow.

When vision is clear,
the mind is at ease
and every apprehension melts away.

In this moment of gentle peace,
I give thanks
for all that has been.

Today, at the crossroads of time,
I welcome with a soft embrace
what is yet to come.

Paradox

Give thanks for thirst.
Give thanks for drink.

Give thanks for hunger.
Give thanks for food.

Give thanks for dark nights.
Give thanks for bright days.

Give thanks for Sister Sun.
Give thanks for Brother Moon.

Imagine the Light

Imagine each moment,
a gratitude day,
a time to give thanks
despite loss and dismay.

Imagine this moment,
a gratitude day,
when your world seems shattered,
torn asunder and grey.

In the midst of laments,
let the light of gratitude in.

Prayer of the Cosmos

The divine presence permeates all life. Each flower, child and cloud signifies the sacredness of all.

We gather as a people called forth by trust, promise and compassion. Standing on the shoulders of those who have gone before, we remember our origins and the company of the mystics and prophets who join us on this journey.

We remember and give thanks to the originating energy of the universe, to the Ancient One of days, whose vast generosity brought us into existence and calls us forth today.

We remember and celebrate the great and noble narrative of the universe, which reveals the depths of the past and the promise of the future, and announces with clarity and hope a profound epiphany at this incarnational moment.

We gather as a holy people, called forth into circles of gratitude and proclamations of trust; we remember the scriptures of creation, those proclamations of divinity are inscribed in the sacred rocks on whose foundation our planet stands.

The shimmering beauty of the trees and flowers is an exaltation of existence, which shines forth in verdant wonder, as rainbows of sacredness manifest everywhere in our midst.

We celebrate also our companions on the way, our cousins of creation, who swim in the oceans, dance in the meadows and soar above us in the sky.

We make our eucharist today, embraced by the members of humanity, who with conscious self-awareness illuminate our paths and show us the way.

We remember now and celebrate the family of ancestral prophets and pilgrims who have been tellers of the story, whose lives we honor, and from whose inspiration we draw strength: Moses, Allah, Confucius, Buddha, Daniel, Mohammed, Isaiah, Ruth, Naomi, Sarah and others.

We honor the preexistent Word, the incarnate One, and Jesus of the cosmos and Earth, who lived among us then and who now permeates, illuminates and makes sacred every moment and molecule of existence.

We remember also those who have named our journey and whose voices challenge and cultivate our lives with monasteries of trust, hope and compassion.

Among those who have gone before, we honor, celebrate and are inspired by Mary, Paul, Elizabeth, Peter, Mary Magdalene, Veronica, John, Luke, Matthew and Mark. We think also of the great cultural workers of yesterday and today, by whose lives we are inspired and who incarnate wisdom for this sacred, defining moment.

We recall the mystics of the past and present: Meister Eckhart, Hildegard of Bingen, Teresa of Avila, John of the Cross, Julian of Norwich, Francis of Assisi, Clare of Assisi, Mechthild of Magdeburg, Dante and so many more.

We gather with deep gratitude and look back to those days

long past, and invite their presence and vision to inspire us and send us forth today.

Among the prophets of yesterday and today are Gandhi, Pope John XXIII, Karl Rahner, Edward Schillebeeckx, Dorothy Day, Teresa of Calcutta, Thomas Merton, Brother David Steindl-Rast, Pierre Teilhard de Chardin, Bede Griffiths, Dom Hélder Câmara, Dr. Martin Luther King, Jr., Gustavo Gutiérrez, Dorothy Stang, Oscar Romero, Elizabeth Johnson, Ilia Delio, Rosemary Radford Ruether, Ursula King, Kateri Tekakwitha, Brother Andre, Mary Mackillop, Barbara Fiand, Gregory Baum, Huston Smith, Margaret Brennan, Jack Egan and the many saints and martyrs anonymously inscribed in the prophetic book of life.

We include the Earth saints from the present and the past who have reminded us to honor and care for our sacred home. Numbered among those who have taught us to be open to the primary revelation of creation, and whose existence has inspired literacy for life: Rachel Carson, Farley Mowat, Thomas Berry, Henry David Thoreau, John Muir, Jane Goodall, Black Elk, Chief Seattle, Loren Eiseley, Annie Dillard, Miriam MacGillis, Brian Swimme, Mary Evelyn Tucker and others.

Mindful of brokenness and beauty all around, we now recall and gather, enveloped in a world of beauty, wonder and belonging, to make our Earth an altar and to give thanks for all that was and is to be.

Conscious of the sacredness of existence—that all is holy and infused with the divine Spirit—we take these simple elements of bread and wine, offspring of Earth, as a sign of each and the communion of all.

Called forth from the heart of the cosmos and planetary beauty all around, we remember the liberating journey of the Exodus, the Passover meal, the promised land and the place that will set all captives free.

Now, inspired by the words inscribed in our tradition and announced by Jesus of the cosmos and the cross, we remember, signify and say, "This is my body."

Also inspired and nourished by the blood of Earth, which irrigates our souls and activates all life, we echo and recall the words of the last supper and together we say, "This is my blood."

Together we proclaim our trust: I believe in the great Paschal moments of the universe, manifest in the galaxies and personified in the Cosmic Christ. I believe in the incarnational energy of the flaring forth, in the cosmic crucifixion of galaxies and stars. I believe in self-transcendence and new life, embodied and expressed in the emergence of Earth, life and humans. I believe in Jesus of Nazareth and in his journey from the manger of Bethlehem, the cross of Gethsemane, the risen mystery of the empty tomb, to transfiguration on Mount Tabor and beyond. I believe in the enveloping mystery of the Cosmic Christ, whose hidden presence, manifest in every sight and sound, announces beauty, wonder and belonging everywhere.

With gratitude and praise, we remember and are inspired to look forward with hope and make our collective acclamation to a future that is unknown.

We remember all who have gone before and anticipate a future filled with abundant life, manifest in every galaxy, species, ancestor and star. We are mindful of every species gone extinct without a resurrection, each life squandered on the battlefields of war.

From our planetary altar, we behold a cosmos and a world alive with divine creative energy, pulsating, transfigured and transformed every day in every way.

Nourished for the journey, we take up our planetary task, embraced by the sacred envelope of life.

Empowered by the universe, we join our words and work with the great cosmic thrust that invites us into a future as yet unknown.

As new people, transfigured and transformed, we join the great eucharistic banquet at the dawn of a new era, infused with cosmic wisdom. Grateful to the God of the cosmos, who invites us into partnership, we go forth to co-create a new world, a new heaven and a new Earth.

To Leonard Cohen

Leonard, where are you?
Yes, you I mean,
the dear, often depressed one
from Montreal.

The balladeer of hope
in the dark.

You who sang alleluia to the world,
to Mary Anne, Sisters of Mercy
and me.

We miss you, Leonard,
on this Jesus Buddha day.

As you exit, Leonard,
let the darkness in.
Alleluia, dear one,
alleluia to the world.

The Kiln of the Divine

Welcome morning's
gentle sunshine,
her cool, crisp breeze.
Earth speaks today
of wondrous beauty.

We gather this morning,
vessels of clay,
shaped, formed and brandished
by the winds and storms of life.

Now healed, warmed and strengthened
in the kiln of God's embrace,
we venture forth again.
Welcome and give thanks
as we await the day.

I Saw Christ Today

I saw Christ today.
Eighteen women and men
filling out applications
to discover a place to call home,
a place of privacy,
of protection from the weather
and of violence in the street.

As I gazed at these seekers,
I thought of Thomas Merton,
who one day in Louisville,
at the corner of Fourth and Walnut,
looked around at those on the street
and was moved to say,
"I loved all those people."

In a similar way, today,
at St. Mary's Center in Oakland,
I looked around the room
at the urban refugees
working on their applications
and felt like Merton many year ago.
I loved everybody.

Communion

God of all creation,
source of love and light,
artist of our fondest dreams,
Your canvas of beauty
shines forth
in this sacred place.

Ancient One
of ancient days,
Your planet pulsates
with heartbeats of beauty,
resonance of love
in many manifestations.

As we celebrate
with awe, wonder and mystery
at this new moment of grace,
we announce the amazing news:
we are all related,
companions of hope,
partners in courage.

Amidst joy and sorrow,
may sacredness remain.

To Rise and Fall, and Begin Again

The undulating dynamic of birth, death and rebirth permeates the fabric of existence. It is true for me and for you, as well.

Born of a father of Irish heritage and a mother with French Canadian roots, my early years found me siding with the outsider and the oppressed. As a young man, I felt a resurgence of energy and engagement with the advent of Vatican Council II, with its emphasis on aggiornamento and its proclamation of the relevance of the church in the modern world. I saw a possibility that marvelous things could happen, as a fresh aliveness flowed into the hearts and minds of many.

In my work with community organization, I saw that people could learn to act freely and achieve what is possible for them to do, as well as make this freedom available for others. Later, when I experienced creation spirituality, another significant dimension of the puzzle fell into place. Through evolutionary science, I began to understand that the events of my life—a reality that is true for all of us—had prepared me for what's next.

A new vehicle for awareness and engagement discovered its place in my soul as I beheld the sequence of a relevant faith, self-deliverance and the ability to act. I rejoiced to discover the journey of the soul in justice. My early inclinations were reaffirmed by the realization that my personal identity could find its fullest expression in work that brings balance, harmony and peace to people and the planet.

I began to experience my life as a Christian in way that healed the division between how I understood my life to be and how I would want it to be. I embraced the realization that God is not an object to be prayed to but rather an enveloping, visible sacred presence that permeates every molecule of existence.

In awakening to the realization of the divine in all things, I was able to contemplate the origins of things and the fourteen-billion-year history that has brought us to where we are now. I could give expression to each new moment of existence as it pulsates among us and draws us into life. It is a life of adventure, risk and the promise of an ever-present now.

To Knock

It's morning again.
Another day awaits us,
a time of goodbyes
and even some hellos.

"Follow your promptings,"
I hear the sacred say.

Now is the time to knock,
to knock fervently
at the doorway of your heart
and discover there,
waiting patiently,
the one for whom you seek.

Summons

Listen deeply to the call,
the call of the wild,
the voice of the Earth.

Listen deeply to the call,
the call of the wounded,
the call of the outsider.

Hear the divine summons.
"Now is the time,"
I hear the invisible one say.

Venture forth
without context or mandate.
Let the hidden one of ancient days
be your compass and your guide.

Tuesday at Sacred Heart

It's Tuesday again.
It's 7:00 PM,
time for bible study
at Sacred Heart.

They trickle in
from workplace and home,
with questions, heartaches,
gentle breezes of joy.

They gaze at their week
through the eyes of faith,
recount "God moments,"
with transparent hope.

They read scripture,
tell stories,
pray together,
then vanish into the night.

Grounded

Find your place,
feel the ground beneath your feet.

Settle down, know why you're here.
Let peace embrace your soul.

Let go, lest what's in your past
hold you back.

Venture forth, my friends.
The future may be more beautiful
than all that went before.

Ripples

Hovering over the waters,
currents of wisdom
stir deeply the channels of our souls,
repel the relentless shores of life.

Ripples of unrest
cascade into awareness.
Waves of wonder
weave fragments of brokenness,
heal the shattered world.

One more time,
celebrate the presence,
the ebb and flow of life.

All That Lies Between

I want to tell you
about joy and pain,
exaltation and sullenness,
and all that lies between.

Shake off the inattentive gaze,
awaken to the moment,
see shadows on the bay.

Thunder breaks the silence from above,
while echoes from the deep
resonate in my soul.

Is this not what I've been waiting for?
An enveloping embrace
of every waking moment.

O Invisible One,
source of love and light,
hear Your people cry
as every broken heart
seeks peace across the land.

Silence Beckons

It's one of those days, I guess.
Nothing seems to work.
The lights went out,
the radio was silenced.
Storms rumbled off the Carolina coast.

Everything is different now,
without light and sound.
A dark silence beckons.
I enter a surprising and sacred place,
a well of wisdom.

Throughout the night,
I listen with my heart.
In the silence and the darkness,
Your presence reappears.

Christmas Day

Yes, it's Christmas.
Silent night salutations
echo across the land.
Gatherings near and far
tell the manger story
of the God child
and the star.

We remember now
that we are not alone.
We are also wrapped
in swaddling clothes,
in the wonder
of this Christmas Day.

The Call to the True Self

Thomas Merton was a person of curiosity and courage. Describing a most powerful moment of prayer, he wrote, "I think for the first time in my whole life I really began to pray—praying not with my lips and with my intellect and my imagination, but praying out of the very roots of my life and of my being, and praying to the God I had never known."

Merton wrote with deep clarity about the immediacy of his personal experience, in a way that was true in his time and remains true to us today. His writings addressed many themes, including personal conversion; mysticism; and issues of war, peace and civil rights. He was an artist, poet, writer and photographer, and his vision was free of any tendency toward sentimentality. He was inspired by the work of Bernard of Clairvaux, who wrote, "You will find something more in woods than in books. Trees and stones will teach you that which you can never learn from masters."

Merton awakened us to the beauty of the natural world. His creative spirit was nourished by the words of Hildegard of Bingen, who wrote, "The person who does good works is indeed this orchard bearing good fruit."

Thomas Merton's enduring appeal comes from his reflection on the call of the true self. He challenges us to be people of an open heart and mind, and encourages us to have an undefended intimate encounter with the divine.

Richard Rohr picks up on this theme in *The Naked Now*, where he writes about the call for the authentic self, undefended and open before God. He invites us to respond to Merton's invitation to become our true self, naked before the divine and untouched by illusion. He urges us to take down the shield of the heart and allow the divine to see us as we truly are. When we are able to do this, we discover that the divine we seek has been there all the time.

Merton embraced the natural world as a source of divine presence. He writes, "The silence of the forest is my bride and the sweet dark warmth of the whole world is my love, and out of the heart of that dark warmth, comes the secret that is heard only in silence." He invites to remain in solitude long enough to emerge as the person we are meant to be.

When we plunge into the deep interiority of our soul, we discover there, beyond any inordinate self-consciousness, the wellspring we dare to call our life.

Soul Signs

Feel the cool breeze
on your face.

Rejoice within the wellspring
of your heart.

Sense fresh energy
rising from below.

Read carefully the wisdom
of your soul.

Listen to the cosmic voice:
you belong here!

You've always belonged here.
Welcome home!

To Be at Home

At home in God,
I sense the rivulets of love
undulating within
my heart and soul,
announcing You are here
at this place of wonder,
where rivers of grace
bubble up gently
in the relentless silence,
sending out ever-widening circles
to the frontiers of my heart.

ENGAGEMENT

I Feel Called

I know that poverty must cease.
I know this through the brokenness
and conflict in my heart.

I know that protest
is my most prophetic act.

I feel called today
to bring people together
to break bread and tell the story.

I feel called today
to listen to the heartbreak of our broken world
and celebrate the wonder of creation.

I feel called today to fall in love,
to feel at home,
to be touched by God.

I feel called
to compose a new paragraph
for life.

New Ways of Engagement

Today I dream of
new ways to be just,
new ways to have mercy,
new ways to have hope,
new ways to listen,
new ways to feel the pain of others and this planet,
new ways to act with the universe in mind,
new ways to become a planetary person,
new ways to speak truth to power,
new ways to be courageous,
new ways to be engaged,
new ways to respond,
new ways to heal,
new ways that are powerful, purposeful and strong,
new ways to renew the face of the Earth.

Thoughts on Our Great Work

When I reflect on what Thomas Berry called the great work, my heart is moved with gratitude for his life and for his vision, which remains with us today.

Thomas reminds us that to participate in the great work is to align our energies with the dynamic, unfolding energy of the universe. When this happens, God's work becomes our work. As we align our personal destiny with the larger destiny of the universe, we are carried into the future by the creative energy of the divine that flows in and through our lives.

Thomas sheds light on his great work by recounting an experience that took place when he was eleven-years-old. One day in May, he ventured beyond the family home to the meadow across the creek. As he gazed at the white lilies and at the clouds in the blue sky, saw the water glistening in the sunshine and listened to the crickets in the meadow, he was moved to ecstasy.

The beauty of this experience touched his soul; it was as if this moment of grace left its sacred imprint on him. From that day forward, his work was guided by a simple principle: What was good for the meadow was good for the world. And what was not good for the meadow was not good for the world and should be avoided.

My own meadow is the St. Clair River—the beautiful body of water that connects Lake Huron and Lake St. Clair in the Great Lakes region. The river bears the name of St. Clare of Assisi because it was discovered on the feast of St. Clare, well known for her love of God's creation.

As a boy, I grew up on the shores of the St. Clair River and learned to swim in, skate on and fish in its sacred waters. It was a poultice for my soul when I was sad and often a source of joy and celebration.

On one occasion, after I had been away from the St. Clair River for some time, as I approached the river, my mouth began to water. As a result, I became aware that I had a cellular relationship with the sacred waters of the St. Clair.

I often think that this body of water can be viewed as a metaphor for what unites us all and holds our world together. This uniting force brings together two countries (Canada and the United States), as well as heaven and earth, God and the world and each individual and the larger community.

When I go to sleep at night, I sometimes remember its beauty as a sacrament of my soul and as a guide for living: That which unites is good; that which separates is not good. This principle informs the great work.

On many occasions, I have invited the participants in classes I taught to reflect on their childhood experiences of nature and to identify their own meadow experiences. They can then trace how their meadow experiences have guided their great work and influenced their destiny in the world. I invite you to do this reflection yourself now.

As we discover the focus of our great work, it also behooves us to think about how we can move away from this time in which humans are devastating the planet and move toward a time when we will be present to the planet in a more mutually enhancing way. Combining our personal work with the larger concerns of our epoch is our common task, our overarching great work.

Good Companions

At this turning point in human/Earth history, we join with good companions on the journey. We sense that we belong to something wider and deeper than we have yet imagined. We listen with new awareness to the hopes and aspirations alive within us. We sense the enduring presence of the divine that continues to speak to us in images, memories and sounds.

We join with others who feel deeply the call to a new life, as each day we die to ourselves and rise to a fresh concern for the Earth and its peoples. Our concern is focused on the work of liberation, freedom and the call to service. It is a call that renders companionship more possible and encounters with the divine more frequent and free.

We take up the challenge and privilege to create together new contexts for freedom. We seek a free space wherein we can become liberated from the oppressive influences of a consumer-driven society that embodies the wounds of race, gender and class conflict and exhibits the increased chasm between the haves and the have nots, the powerful and the powerless.

Companionships provides fresh energy for the transformation of society and enhanced sensitivity for creativity. As good companions on the journey, we move forward together to free ourselves from a culture programmed for relentless economic development and flowing out of imposed patterns of behavior.

Tomorrow We Vote

I see more clearly now,
peering through the marine layer
over San Francisco Bay
this Monday afternoon.

Today my vision becomes clearer
through the fog of news
that scatters truth and wisdom
to the wind.

Today I come home again
to what is just and true,
celebrate life, liberty and the pursuit of happiness
from the halls of democratic peace.

Again I hear the clarion call,
from the streets of California to the halls of Congress.
We say out loud again,
"Today we march, tomorrow we vote."

Ballot Box Surprise

Shelly the dog greets me this morning,
unaware of what just happened.
What happened?
Was that a ballot box surprise?
Did democracy fail us?
Anger and rebellion rule the day.

We gather now, disappointed pilgrims,
plunged into this unexpected hour,
our nation's Gethsemane moment.

In the face of this loss,
this time of disappointment,
this moment of darkness,
we hear a mysterious call for hope,
we search for the light,
we remember friends.

In the midst of goodness and apparent evil,
we find our loving God,
here with us on this Wednesday morning.

I learned a lesson from Alinsky long ago:
there is a positive in every negative.
Out of inevitable darkness, a future dawn is born.

We search for wisdom on this day
as we ponder Sr. Barbara's words:
"The source of everything,
which becomes fully visible

in the human presence of Jesus,
is visible to us through the empowering spirit."

The Fate of Our Country

We are seeing around us now a new order of chaos. Immigrants are faced with deportations that will tear their families apart. Religious organizations are threatened and cemeteries vandalized. The institutions of the government, press and finance are being destabilized. Our foundational principles of democracy are being threatened.

At this critical moment, I ask, how can people who were raised as Christians and Catholics stand by and let such chaos occur? How can they allow freedom and democracy to be at risk?

As I see it, the problem is an old worldview that champions death rather than life.

With this worldview, we believe that God created a perfect world, a place of happiness and eternal reward. We see human death and cultural death as doorways to the rapture and eternal bliss. Theology, fairness, justice and peace have no place in this worldview because they are seen as obstacles to eternal life.

This is *not* the worldview taught by Jesus. He questioned oppression and advocated for the poor. He invited us to become beatitude people. He would caution us not to argue and shout, but rather to listen to and talk with those we oppose. He would ask us to reflect on the principle that the opposition often does the right thing for the wrong reason.

I believe Jesus would find comfort in the peaceful resistance rising up all over the country in response to the Trump effect. We see this in the town halls of elective representatives; in the new movements for justice; and in the actions of those supporting immigrants, Muslims, First Nation's people, the environment and more.

Each day, we have a choice. We can hold onto an old worldview or we can let the divine creative energy burst forth in our souls, dissolve all our rigid thoughts and welcome a future that is filled with zest for life.

Discovery

I want to tell you about discovery,
tell you about who I am,
about what I believe,
about faith, about justice,
about what I hope to say—
whether you believe it or not.

Justice is all I have to say.
When you tell me about sorrow and joy,
about the wound inside,
about organizing as your first act,
about recognizing others,
justice is all I have to say.

Justice making creates good companions
who eat common bread,
consume the food of freedom,
celebrate what is not to be found in books,
peer into silence and solitude.

Discover the wilderness
you dare to call your life.
Describe the scribe of your spirit,
the spirit who guides your uncertain pen
and reveals secrets yet untold.

Privilege

We take up the privileged task
of showering on the hungry, homeless and poor
the fruits of God's creation,
protecting the sacredness of the Earth.

Hunger

The story of engagement unfolds,
fresh alternatives emerge
through our collective aspirations.
We rediscover hope.

We awaken to a new future,
to the beauty and brokenness of life,
and gratefully recall
we are genetically coded for hope.

Pentecost Moment

I have often hoped for and imagined what could be called a planetary Pentecost—a new moment in human/Earth history when we experience a felt sense of renewed energy. That energy blows through the static structures of society and soul, and alerts us to the promise that change is in the air.

We anticipate a time when newness is born and community is possible. We recall the gospel stories that recounted the descent of the spirit. We are consoled and comforted when we consult the scriptures and remember again that it was following the death and resurrection that we experienced the sending of the spirit that now makes it possible for us to take up life's challenges and continue our work.

Through this Pentecost moment, community is formed and a new world is made possible. As we remain open to new opportunities for community and compassion, we look to heal the brokenness of society and the fragments of our lives. My vision is of a dynamic destiny that is always new, one in which people gather to solve their problems and create community, in which the spirit of God is present to guide us into new understandings and new levels of companionship.

GEO-JUSTICE

To Ignite a True Future

As I reflect on my life, with its ebbs and flows, crests and diminishments, I come to its closing pages with a deep and enduring hope, as well as anticipation for the next chapter yet to be lived, designed and co-created.

What I long for is something energizing and real. As best as I can state it, I sense the emergence of something that is entirely new, yet fully rooted in the past. It is a dream of a powerful rebirth of what has inspired us in the past and what we hope to create and cherish.

This future begins with a community of self-aware people who have access to the instruments of cultural genesis, and a revolutionary worldview in which each person wakes up to an entirely new world each day. It is a world in which we are committed to making it possible for all to pursue their true destiny. Empowered by companionship and the ability to act, we move forward to more fully realize what it possible.

People of a common story, we are bound together in a compassionate embrace. We follow the vision of Thomas Berry, who wrote about the original flaring forth that ignited our psychic energies and about how we have been shaped and fired in the same primordial furnace.

As we ignite our sense of the future, we ponder the origin of the universe and the transformational events that have led to this present moment. It is a narrative replete with mystery and meaning, and an awareness that consciousness has been there from the very beginning and is present in each of us from our earliest moment of life.

We embrace the vision of Teilhard de Chardin, who blended Christianity with evolutionary principles. The question we inevitably ask is "What are we going to be and do next?" As we move forward into the next wave of evolution, we echo the wisdom of Teilhard, who proclaimed, "I am a pilgrim of the future on my way back from a journey made entirely in the past."

Thus we take our place as a people paused on the doorway of new beginnings. We are fueled by the enduring impulse to become creators of a new story. This story emerges from the embers of an energy that ignited our imaginations in the past and whose sustaining force remains with us today. It is a renaissance of energy. A psychic spark was ignited in our soul, and from that time on, a new door has been open to the future. We know that tomorrow will be different from today, that we can be delivered to ourselves, that we can break free from the dramas of everyday existence and discover our true destiny.

Our existence is punctuated by the joys and sorrows that prepare each new tomorrow as an opportunity to reach out courageously into the future. After all, we know—in the words of Saul Alinsky—that we're "never going to go back anyway." In our ongoing journey, we retrieve each new moment as a chance to act freely and gain access to what remains yet to be discovered—an engagement that nourishes and transforms. With each passing day, we celebrate the sacredness of a life-enhancing unfolding and meet the future that is struggling to be born.

We listen to the sacred voice summoning us to life and reminding us that integral ecology means our commitment to the natural world cannot be indifferent to social justice. We must embrace each new tomorrow with a holistic understanding that encompasses both beauty as well crises in an inclusive synthesis. We are called forward into a new planetary challenge that invites us to navigate the turbulent waters of contemporary culture and recommit ourselves to fall in love with the dream of a better tomorrow. Together, we fashion this new tomorrow so we can become more alive to nature, culture and ourselves.

What is Justice?

What is justice?
Is it not the great work
of creating the conditions
by which beauty can shine forth?

What is justice?
Is it not dissolving dualism,
nurturing the conditions
that make mutuality possible?

What is justice?
Is it not our acknowledgment of rights,
an equitable distribution
among those acutely in need?

What is justice?
Is it not a willingness to listen,
an ability to act with and on behalf of
those closest to the issue?

What is justice?
Is it not a fusion of consciousness and conscience,
from which flows a capacity for critical reflection,
a context for the transformation of the world?

What is justice?
Is it not engaging the powers of the universe,
and discovering from this new capacity
strategic expressions to transform the world?

What is justice?
Is it not the manifestation of love
through acts of compassion
to heal the face of Earth?

What is justice?
Is it not the spontaneous expressions of vision,
possibility, hope,
the promise of freedom and pathways to peace
through wonder, solidarity and engagement?

Earth, Water and Land

"Nourish this world
with food and drink,"
I hear Lady Wisdom say.

"Listen to the cry
of the poor and the Earth,"
I hear the Sacred One say.

What did your ancestors say?

My father hoed his garden,
brought abundance
to my mother's table.

With red tomatoes, rows of lettuce,
carrots, he joyfully fed his family,
while echoes of famine
drifted through his mind and heart.

Especially the potato shoots
he planted each Good Friday,
a medicine from the famine.

Do you remember, as I do,
summer rains falling
from the far-off sky
to quench the thirst of his seeds?

Yes, the garden was his altar,
moistened by fresh water,

as the blood of Mother Earth quenched
the parched and eager land.

He made his Eucharist each evening
as he walked upon the land
row by row.

Together we say a great amen
to Sr. Dorothy of the Rainforest,
who along with her sister,
stood courageously with a bible in her hand.

She gave her life
and breathed her last
so that the trees could be
the lungs of the Earth.

Let us breathe today
as we celebrate Earth, water and land
on this sacred day.
Amen.

State of the World

Blessed world,
I feel your unrest in my heart.
You perceive the unrest in my heart,
in the hearts of young and old alike.

May we always feel deeply for children,
for the unborn of every species.
"Heal me,"
I hear Earth cry.

Be present to my beauty
and my pain.
Listen to my cry,
"Heal all separation."

"Quench my thirst for justice,"
I hear my mother say.
Now is the time
to heal the unrest in my soul.

Make peace possible.
Savor each new moment.
Let wisdom flow, that I may for the first time
understand what salvation means.

Hear the Cosmos Sing

Tattered and ravaged world,
torn asunder by hunger and strife,
bind up your wounds,
overcome toxins, terror and death.

Let healing happen
in the cosmos
and the soul.
Bring forth newness.

Listen, listen,
hear the cosmos sing:
I am here,
I am alive,
I am home.

Cosmos: A New Monastery Option

Throughout history and the journey named in each of our lives, an enduring theme that marks the human experience is the quest for the living God.

There was a time when people who desired a deep and meaningful experience of the divine chose the monastic option; their motivation was to spend long hours in silence, vigorously read and recite the psalms of sacred texts and engage in physical labor. They were motivated by St. Benedict, who counseled his monks with the mantra "To work is to pray." They were encouraged to view their lives and work as their contribution to ongoing creation, and to see their work as a partnership with the divine, bringing the unfinished universe one more step along the way. This spiritual approach was influenced by a worldview in which God and human, heaven and Earth, were seen as inherently divided.

More recently, borrowing from words of medieval mystic Mechtild of Magdeburg, the approach of panentheism emerged. Mechtild wrote, "The day of my spiritual awakening was the day I saw and knew I saw all things in God and God in all things." With this approach, believing people are able to trust that all of creation contains the signature of God. The division between the imminent and transcendent presence of the divine is dissolved. As a result of panentheism, the transcendent is seen to be present in the imminent.

Encouraged by the prophets of yesterday and today, we take each day as it comes, allowing life to emerge. When we embrace the teaching of Francis of Assisi, we follow a trajectory of wisdom and intuition not found in previously understood patterns of religion and culture. We move forward without any predetermined pathway or clear context to give shape and form to our lives.

The calling of our time is to proceed without naming our life and work according to any preexisting category of the culture, to respond to the divine summons to heal and protect the Earth and the people of the Earth. The challenge is simply to pray our way into the future. This call is not mandated by any institutional structure, but simply by the promptings of the spirit and the cry of the Earth and its people. Each of us is invited to consider what is still possible for us to do.

Resacralizing the Earth

I have often been troubled by the way some Christians seem compelled to live in two different worlds. One is a world in which God resides; the other is a world in which humanity dwells and God is absent. Theologians call this latter view of the world theism.

A friend expressed this kind of split awareness by saying, "We pray to God on Sunday, and we prey on our neighbor on Monday."

Such an approach removes the sensitivity we would need to care for our common home, the Earth. Pope Francis wrote in his encyclical that such an attitude can lead to "a throw-away culture." And he wrote on Twitter that "The Earth, our home, is beginning to look more and more like an immense pile of filth."

With the Pope—as well as Teilhard de Chardin, Thomas Berry and others—as our guides, we see that another way is possible.

When we embrace evolution, something amazing happens. We are infused with God's creative energy as we become aware that the divine has been present since the beginning of the universe. Suddenly, every person, plant and tree is seen to be infused with God's energy. Every child, elder, puppy and kitten is understood to be sacred and soaked in God.

The lyrics of "Holy Now" take on new meaning. The birds' songs become a verse from scripture, while rivers and streams become holy. All of creation is now the locus of divine presence.

When we awaken to the realization that God is present in all things, we are energized to take up our privileged task of resacralizing the Earth.

World Made New

Engage in works of mercy,
gentle acts of trust.
Practice forgiveness,
do what is just.

Surround both friend and foe
with circles of compassion.
Allow healing to happen.

Illuminate my soul
that I may see
the world made new.

Eco-Feminism

The old patriarchal worldview reinforced the dualism that proclaimed men as the recipients of the supernatural grace of thinking, and relegated women to the natural grace manifest as intuition and service. Such a distorted worldview can no longer be the foundation of sustainable life on planet Earth.

Historically, religious women were the creators of culture as they served in schools, hospitals and social agencies. Today new initiatives have emerged on the frontiers of society and church. Miriam Therese MacGillis has been one prophetic voice through her work at Genesis Farm in New Jersey, where she provides programs on Earth literacy, the universe story and community supported agriculture.

Every two years, the Sisters of Earth gather to inform and support each other in the great work of creating a mutually enhancing world for humanity and Earth. Their lives are nourished as they create community to celebrate the poetry of existence. Their ecological awareness overflows into engagement on issues of gender, justice, race, poverty and care for creation. They take their place as animators of the ecological age as they venture into the transitional moment Joanna Macy calls "the great turning."

People of faith can now proclaim, "Whatever befalls the people of Earth befalls the daughters of Earth." The term for this new awakening is *eco-feminism*. This prophetic insight has alerted us to a fresh awareness that the oppression of Earth and the oppression of women are integrally connected.

A Disastrous Choice

As expected, President Trump removed the United States from participation in the Paris Climate Accord. This decision was based on greed and on adherence to what is most dangerous to the well-being of our fragile planet. Such an act stands in opposition to what is most prophetic in America.

This outrageous choice makes no economic or planetary sense. It contradicts the best of the scientific and social visionaries alive today. It disregards all of Al Gore's climate change initiatives, and places the future of our planet and its people in greater jeopardy. It ignores Johanna Macy's vision of the great turning. It makes Thomas Berry's dream of the Earth become instead a nightmare for humanity. The fact that the very day of Trump's withdrawal from the Paris Accord fell on the eighth anniversary of Thomas's passing is ironic, to say the least.

I can feel the pain of this disastrous choice. Yet, as I contemplate the significance of this moment, I nevertheless look for reasons to feel encouraged. I think about the sun's generous gift, about the beauty of the flower outside my window, about the spontaneity of the child who lives with her parents down the hall.

And especially, I am inspired by the numerous people who gather here and around the country, motivated by genuine love for the Earth. These people are our hope for the future. They are dedicated to preserving the sacredness of life, so that future generations may live in a truly participatory democracy, where people recognize and listen to one another.

They dream of a world whose first act is compromise and whose organization is founded on justice making.

The toxic news of the day may assail me, but I also cannot ignore the goodness of the people I see around me. I feel hopeful seeing something precious and new bubbling up at a grassroots level. I pray that the future will more just, that people will be more engaged, that our journey together will continue and that our tomorrows will be better than all our pasts.

An Economy in Which People Matter

There is an old story that a reporter asked the billionaire John D. Rockefeller, "How much money is enough?" and the answer came back "One more dollar!" There are various versions of this tale, and we don't know for certain that any of them are true. But the point is still taken.

I've always been a fan of country music, and I especially like the song "A Satisfied Mind," written by Joe Red Hayes and Jack Rhodes, and made famous by Ella Fitzgerald, Bob Dylan and Porter Wagoner, among others. Hayes said he wrote the song after his father-in-law asked him to name the richest man in the world. His father-in-law said all his answers were wrong: the richest man was the one with a satisfied mind. In fact, money can't buy what we most value in life, and not one rich person in ten has a satisfied mind, as the song tells us.

One glance at the news today, and it is difficult not to be overwhelmed by the pain, poverty and homelessness affecting people in many cultures and countries around the world. As I write this, only 5 percent of the population in Puerto Rico has electricity almost two weeks after the hurricane. More than half are without drinking water. Yet the president of this nation is comfortably ensconced at his golf course. The question that comes to my mind is: do we have a culture and an economy in which people matter?

Pope Francis offers his critique of the global economy when says we have made money our god. He laments that while people will die of starvation tonight, food is reserved only for those who are able to pay for it. We consider a drop in the stock market to be "a tragedy," he says, while homeless people dying in the streets is not newsworthy. The economy, he says, "should not be a mechanism for accumulating goods, but rather the proper administration of our common home." I am reminded of Schumacher's words when I hear Pope Francis tell us to "put the economy at the service of peoples."

Nevertheless, there are ministers on the airways today who preach a so-called prosperity gospel proclaiming that if the economy rewards you in this world, you will be assured of God's reward in the next. It is ironic that many who follow this gospel are themselves poor. Instead of seeking a satisfied mind, or seeking to become planetary people who care for the needs of the Earth and its peoples, their highest striving is for "one more dollar."

I suggest that we foster the growth of an economy that can transform objects into subjects, guilt and grief into gratitude, and isolation into love. Only if we start from the premise that the Earth and its people matter, can we begin to discover how much—of what we have, and what we want and what we need—is enough.

Our Great Flaring Forth

From the fireball of our origin,
we discover within
opaqueness and pain,
but also newfound passion
to heal our broken world.

Breaking out of structures
of conformity and pathos,
we fashion fresh motifs of transformation,
cry out with the chorus of creation,
in which every voice of God is heard.

Earth Speaks

Let Earth speak
tales of primary revelation,
stories about the wonder of it all
and the gifts of God's creation.

We view the rocks, water and trees
not as objects to be looked at,
rather as subjects to be communed with.

When we encounter creation,
we activate a deep connection
between the recesses of our soul
and the far reaches of the universe.

With Meister Eckhart,
we joyfully proclaim,
"Every creature is a book about God."

Stirred to our depths,
we are startled by a fresh awareness
of the galaxies within,
those amazing wellsprings we dare call our life.

We honor and give thanks
for those wild and wonderful
manifestations of divinity.

As people, now liberated
from the autism of illiteracy,
we are thrilled to awaken to

the language of the Earth.

We savor the divine presence
that permeates every molecule
of existence.

With "fresh energy and a zest for life,"
we welcome the divine,
which we cannot see, feel, hear, taste or touch,
yet which is fully present in everything.

We awaken to the great and glorious pattern
that connects and hugs us
in a divine embrace.

With each passing day,
we more and more cherish
our companions of creation
who join us on the journey.

With great thanks,
we give voice to our experience
of the primary revelation.

A Life Restored

We live today in a world too often closed off to intimacy and compassion, a world of isolation, loneliness and misguided mysticism.

It is a world without equity; a world of a great divide; a world of distance and separation; an apartheid world that divides the young and the elderly, the haves and the have nots. It is a world closed off from wisdom, possibility and hope.

It is a world that hovers on the precipice of discouragement, where our mood and motivation reflect a tendency toward isolation and the propensity to settled for an unlived life.

In the face of all our discouragement and loss, something new is stirring—a voice that invites us to embrace a new openness and create a meaningful life.

In this restored life, we will be rewarded with just wages and have a nurturing family in which love, respect and encouragement mark each day. In this life, we will care for the most in need among us; we will feed the hungry, house the homeless and heal the wounds of the neglected and abused.

The world we envision gives courage and support to those who strive to be ecologically sensitive and socially just. We will, when possible, grow our own food. We will support sustainable agriculture and a healthy planet with fresh water, pure air and wholesome land.

Restoration

What do you want to tell us, Earth?
We humans, I mean,
who walk upon your face,
so replete with cosmic beauty.
You have many lessons to share,
burdens we must bear.

I join in your sorrow
for the children who tonight
will die of hunger,
sorrow for the lobotomies of extraction
that ravage your mountain tops
and leave an ugly scar.

I pray today for the compost of your soul,
the genesis of a great Easter moment
when you will be restored,
and all your offspring
will once again rise up in gentle beauty
to sanctify a better day.

About the Author

Jim Conlon was born in Canada in 1936. He received a degree in chemsity from Assumption University of Windsor, and later in theology from the University of Western Ontario, and a PhD from Union Institute and Graduate School. Deeply moved by the impact of the second Vatican Council, the civil rights movement, and the Vietnam War, Jim moved from pastoral work to the streets. Today he is one of the leading teachers of the new narrative of the cosmos. Visit him online at www.jimconlon.net and on Facebook at www.facebook.com/becomingplanetarypeople.

Also Available from Jim Conlon

Becoming Planetary People
ISBN: 978-0-9964387-0-4

Geo-Justice
ISBN: 978-0-9964387-2-8

www.ingramcontent.com/pod-product-compliance
Lightning Source LLC
Chambersburg PA
CBHW071902290426
44110CB00013B/1247